MORE MONEY, MORE LIFE

For my incredible dad

I love you more than words can say. Thank you for showing me the way, for giving me the signposts and for instilling in me the courage and urgency to forge my own path.

When you left us too soon at 58, a fierce determination ignited within me, to stop drifting on the wimds of hope and start pursuing the life I was truly meant to live.

This book, and the *More Money, More Life* it champions, is my heartfelt homage to you. You are, and always will be, my guiding star.

MORE MONEY, MORE LIFE

Every woman's guide to breaking free from money worries and funding your dreams

SARAH BENNETT-NASH

WATKINS
1893

More Money, More Life
Sarah Bennett-Nash

This edition first published in the UK and USA in 2026
by Watkins, an imprint of Watkins Media Limited
Unit 11, Shepperton House, 89-93 Shepperton Road
LondonN1 3DF

enquiries@watkinspublishing.com

10 9 8 7 6 5 4 3 2 1

Designed and typeset by JCS Publishing Ltd.
Printed and bound in the United Kingdom by CPI Group Ltd

The manufacturer's authorised representative in the EU for product safety is:
eucomply OÜ - Pärnu mnt 139b-14, 11317 Tallinn, Estonia,
hello@eucompliancepartner.com, www.eucompliancepartner.com

A CIP record for this book is available from the British Library

ISBN: 978-1-83681-031-5 (Paperback)
ISBN: 978-1-83681-032-2 (eBook)

www.watkinspublishing.com

CONTENTS

INTRODUCTION

Welcome to a new way of thinking about wealth. *More Money, More Life* is your roadmap to redefining your success, so you can break free from financial struggles, and create a life that radiates purpose, joy and abundance. I'll take you on a transformative journey from self-awareness to empowered action, guiding you to align your finances with your values and build a legacy of lasting wealth and well-being.

This isn't about chasing money, working harder or hustling longer; it's about rewriting your relationship with money so financial success flows naturally from who you are and what you truly value.

Following is a breakdown of what you can expect as you journey through this book. With every chapter, you'll gain the tools, mindset shifts and strategies you need to break free from financial struggle, fund your dreams and leave a lasting legacy of prosperity for the people you love.

Section 1: Awareness

Before we can create a life of financial abundance, we need to understand the stories we tell ourselves about money. This section is all about diving deep into your money mindset, uncovering the beliefs holding you back and rewriting the narrative to reflect empowerment, possibility and purpose.

Chapter 1: My money story

We're starting this journey together with a peek into my own money story; the wins, the struggles and the lightbulb moments that changed everything. I invite you to reflect on your own financial history, uncover the beliefs and behaviours shaping your decisions, and begin the mindset shift toward building wealth on your terms.

Chapter 2: The psychology of money

This chapter explores the emotional and psychological aspects of money, blending behavioural finance insights with actionable tools to create wealth intentionally. We'll discusses how personal experiences and global events shape our financial DNA and reactions to money. Here I share my own "money script" inherited from my family, marked by financial tension and my father's unspoken financial stress, which profoundly impacted my own relationship with money and self-worth. A pivotal crisis, being scammed by a builder, became a catalyst for confronting these inherited patterns and redesigning my life.

Chapter 3: Abundance unlocked

This is where awareness meets action. Using the Triple A Framework (Awareness, Alignment and Action), you'll learn how to evaluate your financial health and make smart, purposeful changes that align with your vision of abundance.

Section 2: Alignment

Money should never feel like a grind. In this section, you'll learn how to align your finances with your unique values, purpose and life vision, create authentic goals and design systems that make building wealth feel effortless and empowering.

Chapter 4: Money, meaning & Ikonic Wealth

Your relationship with money reflects your relationship with yourself. This chapter shows you how to align your self-love with your financial vision, uncover your core values and set goals that are as meaningful as they are achievable. It's time to ditch the hustle and embrace abundance with clarity and confidence.

Chapter 5: Build your Evergreen Wealth Engine

Your money should work for you, not the other way around. Here, I'll introduce you to the Evergreen Wealth Engine, a proven framework to help you create new income streams, automate your finances and build a sustainable path to long-term freedom.

Chapter 6: Your magnet for more money

This chapter reveals how you can shift from chasing opportunities to attracting them by building an authentic personal brand that acts as an irresistible force for financial flow. This isn't about superficial branding but about consciously engineering influence and becoming a sought-after authority in your field. I'll show you how to use the six-pillar IKONIC™ Framework (Impact-Driven Identity, Knowledge-Driven Credibility Engine, Opportunity Architecture, Narrative Power, Influence at Scale, Consistency that Converts) to build systematically your Ikonic, authoritative brand.

Section 3: Action

In this final section, you'll learn how to turn your vision into legacy. This is where your dreams come to life. You'll take bold, intentional actions to build momentum, protect your wealth and create a ripple effect of abundance that uplifts your family, your community and beyond.

Chapter 7: The art of execution

Dreams don't just happen, they're built. In this chapter, we'll dive into the MORE framework (Motivation, Obstacles, Resources, Execution), equipping you with tools to turn your ideas into reality. You'll discover the power of joyful habits, progress tracking and the magic to bring your vision to life with ease.

Chapter 8: Protecting your legacy

Wealth isn't just about what you earn, it's about what you preserve. This chapter breaks down essentials like wills, trusts and power of attorney in a way that's simple, empowering and crystal clear. By protecting your legacy, you ensure that your wealth works for you and the people you care about most, long after you're gone.

Chapter 9: Legacy in motion

Your wealth doesn't just support you, it supports the ones you love. From teaching your kids about money to planning for education, retirement and multigenerational wealth, this chapter shows you how to create a family financial plan that aligns with your deepest values and dreams. It's about building a future where every financial decision reflects love, intention and the legacy you want to leave behind.

Chapter 10: Igniting your constellation

Wealth is at its most powerful when it's shared. In this final chapter, you'll discover how to leverage the power of community: building connections, fostering relationships and amplifying your impact. By empowering others, you'll create a legacy of generosity and prosperity that uplifts not just you, but everyone around you.

More Money, More Life is more than just a guide, it's a movement. An invitation to rise up, own your power and live abundantly on your terms. By the end of the book I want you not just to be thinking about wealth, but actively creating it, building a legacy that inspires others. My ultimate aim is to help you step boldly into a life where wealth fuels dreams, uplifts loved ones and leaves a lasting positive indelible mark on the world.

CHAPTER 1
MY MONEY STORY

On my 46th birthday, I felt it. An undeniable, goosebump-inducing shift deep within me. A whisper, soft yet powerful, telling me it was time. Time for something bigger. Something bolder. Something that truly resonated with the core of who I was. It wasn't just a fleeting thought, more a profound calling. A calling for a transformation I could no longer ignore, a call to redefine what "more" truly meant in my life.

From the outside, my life looked flawless, enviable even. A thriving career that ticked all the conventional success boxes. A steady, impressive income. The kind of "Instagram-perfect" existence society applauds. But beneath that glossy surface, I was crumbling. The relentless corporate grind hadn't just tired me, it had systematically drained my joy. The highs that once felt thrilling became fleeting dopamine hits, and the lows lingered, heavy and oppressive, like guests who'd overstayed their welcome and, frankly, trashed the place.

Deep down, in that quiet space where truth resides, I knew this wasn't the life I was meant to live. This wasn't the definition of success I wanted for myself, not anymore. That day, staring at my reflection, seeing the stark disconnect between the outer show and the inner reality, I made a decision. A powerful choice that wasn't just about wanting more; it was about consciously claiming it. The time for a life filled with more purpose, more joy, more freedom was unequivocally NOW.

To be clear, this wasn't some cinematic "Aha!" moment, perfectly packaged and delivered on a silver platter. This decision, this deep knowing, had been brewing for years. I'd spent years waking up on autopilot, going through the motions, a nagging question echoing in my mind: *"Is this really it? Is this what a rich life is supposed to feel like?"*

I'd diligently ticked all the societal boxes, followed the well-worn path to what the world deems "success". Elite school, honours degree, prestigious law qualifications and a US Broker Dealer registration? Double check. A relentless climb up the corporate ladder, racking up promotions like achievements in a game I no longer wanted to play? Check, check, check. On paper, I had it all – the list of qualifications was endless, a credential for practically every step of my career. I was the epitome of the "good girl", the model of achievement. From the outside looking in, it seemed I had conquered the world.

Yet, beneath that polished exterior, a persistent disquiet hummed. A deep, undeniable yearning for something more, something authentic, something real. This wasn't about chasing more zeros in the bank account or indulging in extravagance for its own sake; it was a desperate, soul-deep pursuit of purpose. I craved a life where my daily actions resonated with my core values, where my work was an authentic expression of who I am, and where my days were filled with genuine connection, profound fulfilment and an expansive sense of freedom. I yearned for a life that didn't just look impressive in a boardroom or on a résumé, but felt absolutely incredible in the quiet moments, in the very depths of my heart. I wasn't just tired of emotionally scraping by, I was done. Completely and utterly finished with it.

I yearned for a life that didn't just look impressive in a boardroom or on a résumé, but felt absolutely incredible in the quiet moments

I wanted to feel truly alive again. To have the time and presence to cherish moments with my little ones. To wake up each day feeling not just in control, but empowered, the architect of my life and my future. I wanted a life that was wholly, unapologetically mine. I wasn't just hungry for this change; I was starving for it. But the inevitable question loomed: when the weight of it all feels so overwhelming, where do I even begin to craft this new reality?

Determined to reclaim my life and find that starting point, I dove headfirst into the world of personal development. Workshops, conferences, coaching sessions, seminars … if it promised a pathway to learn, grow and transform, I was there, front and centre, pen in hand, ready to absorb every insight.

Those spaces were electric. You could literally feel the buzz in the air. A potent mix of ambition, hope and a collective belief that transformation wasn't just a distant possibility; it was an absolute inevitability. For the first time in what felt like an eternity, I was surrounded by people who were truly awake. People actively peeling back the layers of societal conditioning, courageously stepping into their inherent power. It was infectious. And in that vibrant, supportive energy, I began to rediscover the essence of who I truly was beneath all the titles, the roles and the never-ending weight of external expectations.

Then I turned my focus to financial seminars, expecting that same electrifying energy and holistic approach to creating a better life. And the vibe just … flatlined. The excitement, the deep connection to a bigger "why" vanished. It was replaced by something that felt cold, sterile and profoundly incomplete. There were absolutely plenty of strategies, formulas, spreadsheets and blueprints for building wealth. But a crucial element was glaringly absent. Something vital was missing from their equation of "more".

The toxicity of financial conversations

The speakers at these financial events were overwhelmingly male, and the conversations disappointingly narrow. It was a relentless echo chamber of numbers and sales tactics. Money in, money out, rinse and repeat. A purely transactional loop that felt devoid of the human element, of the life that money is supposed to serve.

The prevailing vibe was pure "eat what you kill" – in this world, your ability to "hunt" for opportunities and "capture" them directly dictated your financial "meal". This fostered a high-stakes, often brutal environment where success was loudly celebrated, but the inevitable stumbles meant an immediate hit to your income, a precarious existence much like that of our hunter-gatherer ancestors. Crucial aspects of our human experience – balance, burnout, the emotional rollercoaster that often accompanies the pursuit of wealth – weren't just overlooked, they were practically taboo. Purpose, fulfilment and holistic well-being, the very pillars of a *More Money, More Life* existence, were ghosts at their feast. The entire atmosphere felt cold, purely transactional, a million miles away from the soul-stirring, transformational dialogue I knew was possible and desperately craved.

Then there was the deafening silence, the glaring void where female voices should have been. The stages were dominated by men, and this stark imbalance was more than just disappointing; it was profoundly disheartening, and it amplified the deep disconnect I was already feeling. That staggering $1.2 trillion gender wealth gap isn't just a statistic, some abstract number on a page. In those rooms, it became tangible, personal. It was the subtle yet suffocating feeling of being sidelined, of our female perspectives and experiences being rendered invisible in conversations that were supposedly about success, opportunity and creating possibility for all. A relentless thought echoed in my mind – *this has to change, we deserve better than this.*

And then, in a moment of electrifying clarity, a true lightning bolt, it hit me. If I wanted to see a different narrative, a story where money conversations were inclusive, empowering and deeply connected to a life of purpose and joy, I couldn't afford to wait. Waiting for the system to evolve could take decades I didn't have. I would have to create it.

I could no longer be a passive observer, sitting on the sidelines hoping someone else would rewrite the script. If the existing tables didn't offer a seat for women like me, for voices like mine, then I needed to design and build a whole new table. A table where everyone felt welcome, seen and empowered. It was my time to step up, to claim my space and to become the kind of role model I'd been searching for, to be the voice I'd yearned to hear in all those rooms that felt closed off to me and so many others.

But before I could dream of guiding anyone else toward their *More Money, More Life*, before I could help them rewrite their financial narratives, I had to confront the elephant in my room. My own tangled, often messy money story, a complex tapestry woven with threads of fear, scarcity and shame. This wasn't just my story; it was a narrative passed down through generations, its echoes subtly influencing my decisions, my habits and my deepest beliefs about wealth and worth. To authentically light the path for others, I first had to courageously untangle and rewrite my own.

The money script I inherited

Growing up, money wasn't simply a tool in my life; it was a live wire. A source of intense household tension, explosive arguments and heavy, suffocating silences. Money carried an emotional charge that shaped my earliest understanding of worth, security and fear.

My father's premature death at just 58, worn down by a financial stress he never voiced, became a devastating turning point. After he was gone, my sister and I uncovered the heartbreaking reality – piles of unopened bills, ominous demand letters from banks … His silent battle with money wasn't just a personal tragedy; it was a stark, painful wake-up call for me. It wasn't solely about the debt, but also the crushing shame that had enveloped him and barricaded him from seeking help, convincing him he had to bear the crushing weight alone.

And that shame, I realized, didn't die with him. It had insidiously seeped into my own being, twisting the way I viewed money and, more profoundly, the way I saw myself and my own capabilities. No matter how much I earned – my career was "successful" by every external metric – a deep-seated feeling of "not enough" haunted me. Money would flow into my accounts, only to slip through my fingers with alarming speed, as if repelled by an invisible force. The fear of scarcity, of it all disappearing, became a relentless shadow I couldn't outrun, no matter what my income.

On the outside, our family projected an image of abundance. Private schools, luxury cars, a fairy-tale manor house that could have graced a magazine cover. But behind those curated walls, the reality was a turbulent landscape of financial anxiety. Money arguments weren't occasional flare-ups; they were a grim routine. And these heated discussions often escalated to frightening levels. I vividly remember the day my mother's frustration boiled over – she hurled a pot of scalding water at my dad, the contents shattering the kitchen window. My friends later joked about the tinfoil patch that became a semi-permanent fixture, but for me, it was a visceral, daily reminder of money's destructive power when mishandled and steeped in unresolved emotion. Their eventual divorce was protracted, bitter and financially devastating for both. My father never truly recovered his footing, and my mother eventually burned through her settlement, forced to sell the home he'd bought for her just to stay afloat.

This pattern, this inherited money script of instability, wasn't unique to my parents. It echoed the story of my grandparents, who once experienced a life-altering windfall from the football pools, only to find themselves back at square one just a few short years later. It felt like a curse, as if financial insecurity was woven into our family's very DNA, an unbreakable cycle passed down through generations.

And here's a critical piece of understanding I later gained. Money isn't just a numbers game; it's an emotional legacy. Groundbreaking psychological research, such as studies by Yehuda & Bierer on epigenetics, shows how trauma and its associated stresses can, in effect, be passed down biologically, altering how genes express themselves in subsequent generations. Pervasive scarcity thinking, deep-seated shame around wealth (or lack thereof) and a constant fear of loss often don't even originate from our own direct experiences. They can be echoes from our lineage. As Dr Gabor Maté powerfully explains, unresolved emotional pain, particularly from early life or ancestral trauma, can manifest in adulthood as self-sabotaging behaviours or chronic insecurity, including how we interact with our finances. These subconscious patterns and invisible scripts shape how we earn, spend, save and feel about money, often operating entirely beneath our conscious awareness. Until we consciously interrupt this cycle, we risk replaying inherited financial dramas that were never truly ours to begin with. And this was absolutely playing out full force in my life.

Money isn't just a numbers game; it's an emotional legacy

My father's silent financial struggles, the shame that suffocated him, became more than just a tragic memory. It transformed into a profound, albeit harsh, lesson. It was a glaring spotlight on how shame can isolate you, convincing you that you're utterly alone in your struggles. That same inherited shame had been whispering its toxic narrative to me for years, driving me to work harder, be smarter, achieve more, all in a desperate attempt to outrun the fear. And yet, no matter the promotions, no matter the income, I never felt truly safe. Never genuinely secure. I never, ever felt like I was enough.

This was the undeniable reality of my "money story". The intense stress and anxiety surrounding money that had been so loud and palpable in my childhood home hadn't just disappeared; it had shape-shifted and woven itself into the fabric of my adult existence. That realization was a pivotal moment. It was a painful, yet incredibly clarifying unveiling. The source of so much of my adult financial unease was a direct echo from my past. And with that dawning awareness came the first flicker of hope; if a script could be learned, it could also be unlearned and rewritten.

The time for more is NOW

The echoes of my inherited money script, the raw understanding of the fear and scarcity that had shadowed my family for generations, culminated in a single, defiant moment. That day, on my 46th birthday, staring into the mirror, I wasn't just seeing my reflection; I was seeing the potential for a future I was finally ready to claim. I made a promise to the woman looking back at me, a woman I was determined to fully become. The shame would not define me. Fear would no longer call the shots.

"The time for more, more joy, more freedom, more peace, is unequivocally NOW!" I declared, a surge of conviction cutting through years of doubt. This wasn't just a wish. It was a decision. It was time to shatter the cycle, to break free from the autopilot existence, and to consciously architect a life that felt intentional, deeply aligned with my soul and profoundly fulfilling. I didn't just want this transformation; I needed it with every fibre of my being. And I was fiercely committed to doing whatever it took.

Flashback to where my so-called "financial education" began … Wall Street, New York. My first day at Goldman Sachs felt like being dropped onto the set of a high-octane movie. The trading floor was a symphony of controlled chaos. A whirlwind of shouts, rapid-fire movements and an electric energy that pulsed through the very air. Traders bellowed orders, markets shifted with breathtaking speed and multi-million-dollar deals were sealed in seconds.

It was an intoxicating blend of exhilaration and sheer terror, the kind of intense environment that shakes you to your core and leaves you wide-eyed, marvelling at how you even got there. The stakes were astronomical, the ambition palpable. This was Wall Street in all its gritty, demanding glory. In that crucible, I forged resilience, cultivated grit and learned to thrive under immense pressure. I mastered quick decision-making and embraced the relentless pursuit of excellence. It was a bootcamp for my professional identity. Yet, even as my corporate career ascended, the deep cracks in my personal relationship with money began to widen beneath the polished surface.

Despite the promotions and pay raises, and climbing higher on that coveted corporate ladder, the old, inherited money story still had me in its grip. That insidious narrative whispered that wealth could only be earned through relentless toil, endless sacrifice and a constant, anxious striving. Superficially, this belief fuelled my ambition, pushing me to work harder, stay later and aim ever higher. But underneath, it trapped me in a draining cycle of scarcity thinking. No matter how much I earned, it was never, ever enough.

I had mastered the complex art of making money, but I was utterly clueless about how to keep it, let alone grow it or make it work for me. Each pay cheque seemed to evaporate almost on arrival, a frustrating pattern that directly mirrored the financial chaos of my upbringing. So, I did what I thought I had to do. I worked even harder, climbed even higher, desperately trying to out-earn my deep-seated insecurities. But no matter the altitude, I couldn't break free from the invisible shackles of perceived financial instability.

And then, the universe delivered a crisis that would become my most profound catalyst.

I was devastatingly scammed by a builder. I'd handed over not just my hard-earned savings, but my trust, to someone who callously shattered both. I was left on the brink of financial ruin. My apartment, once filled with dreams of renovation, looked like a war zone, stripped bare. My bank account was wiped clean. And I was staring at an impending maternity leave with a tidal wave of dread threatening to pull me under.

It was a moment of sheer, gut-wrenching panic, the kind that forces you to question the very foundations of your life. For years, I'd nurtured a dream of escaping the corporate grind, a vision I'd even named "Project OB40" (Out By 40). It was my quiet plan to build a life of freedom, on my own terms. But now, with the cold reality of financial urgency breathing down my neck, that dream violently shifted from a "someday, nice-to-have" to an immediate, non-negotiable must-have.

This wasn't just a financial setback; it was a brutal, soul-shaking wake-up call. It forced me to hit pause, to finally turn and confront the shadows I'd been running from and to interrogate the very core of my existence with unflinching honesty. I asked myself:

- What toxic money story am I still unconsciously telling myself?
- What deeply ingrained beliefs are holding me captive in this cycle of fear and lack?
- How do I finally rewrite this narrative and claim my financial sovereignty and well-being?

That crisis, as painful as it was, became my crucible. It forged a new level of resilience within me and ignited the courage to finally confront the tangled web of fears, inherited habits and limiting beliefs that had kept me tethered to a life that felt increasingly inauthentic. It sparked the clarity and fierce determination I needed to architect a completely new path, a new plan for my life that I could pour my heart into; one that promised not just financial recovery, but genuine excitement, creative fulfilment and the space to finally have fun on my journey. This new plan wasn't just about spreadsheets and targets; it was about designing a life rich in purpose, passion and playful exploration, where my work would energize me and allow me to contribute meaningfully.

In that defining moment of clarity born from chaos, I made a powerful choice. I refused to let financial fear dictate my future any longer. I refused to allow the shame of my past or the crippling doubts of my present to extinguish the fire of aspiration that still burned within me. I channelled every ounce of my being, my resilience, my newfound clarity, into building a business from the ground up, a vehicle designed not only for my own liberation but for the empowerment of others, helping them design lives of purpose and freedom. Simultaneously, I was plotting my own escape from the gilded cage of corporate life. It was far from easy; it was a relentless, often exhausting battle, a testament to the indomitable power of the human spirit when fuelled by a compelling "why".

It took immense courage to confront those deeply ingrained beliefs that had kept me stuck in patterns of self-sabotage. It demanded dedicated intention to dismantle the old habits that no longer served my vision for a brighter future. And above all, it required a profound commitment to completely redefine what wealth truly meant to me.

I had to rewrite my money story from the foundation up. Through my inner work, a voracious appetite for genuine financial literacy (the kind they don't teach you in school) and a daily commitment to choose growth over fear, I learned to release my suffocating scarcity mindset: that constant, gnawing feeling of not having enough. I began, intentionally, to cultivate and embrace a life of true abundance. I stopped viewing money as a source of stress and started seeing it for what it could be – a powerful tool for creating freedom, impact, purpose and profound joy.

Fast forward eight years, and the landscape of my life is almost unrecognizable from that place of fear and desperation. Today, I'm the founder of two businesses that I absolutely adore, enterprises that not only fuel my passions but also allow me to make a meaningful, positive impact on the lives of others. I spend my days engaged in work that genuinely lights me up, surrounded by inspiring individuals, and empowered by the priceless freedom to design my own schedule and cherish precious time with my little ones. But the most significant transformation, the one that underpins all the others, is this – I've completely and irrevocably rewritten my money story.

I've learned, deep in my bones, that true wealth isn't measured solely by the numbers in a bank account. It's about the richness of aligning your financial life with your deepest values. It's about consciously using money as a dynamic tool to create the life you genuinely desire, rather than being controlled by it. It's about breaking free from the shackles of fear of scarcity, and stepping boldly into an expansive space of possibility, purpose and personal empowerment. This is the essence of living a *More Money, More Life* existence.

I've learned, deep in my bones, that true wealth isn't measured solely by the numbers in a bank account

Your money story starts here

Every single one of us carries a money story. It's like an invisible script running in the background of your life, subtly shaping your choices, driving your behaviours, fuelling your deepest fears and silently steering your entire future.

These powerful stories aren't consciously authored by us, they're inherited. Passed down through our families, absorbed from our culture and imprinted by our earliest environments. And these unexamined money stories, the ones we've accepted without question, are precisely the narratives that can hold us captive, chaining us to familiar patterns of struggle, from living pay cheque to pay cheque, to the exhausting cycle of hustle and burnout. But here's the empowering truth for you. That inherited code, the one that perhaps kept you feeling safe yet left you yearning for something more, doesn't have to be your final programme. You absolutely can break free from the grip of old patterns, from the silent imprisonment of a script that was never truly yours to begin with.

Consider this book your official permission slip, your practical playbook, to courageously challenge the beliefs, habits and subconscious programming that have kept you feeling stuck, perhaps looping on repeat. We're not here to simply slap a budget on top of a broken mindset. We're embarking on a far more profound journey to rewrite your entire money story from the inside out, crafting one that resonates deeply with your authentic truth, your core values and your unique vision of abundance. You're going to discover that this journey isn't just about money. Far from it. It's about what money, when aligned with your soul, can unlock. Genuine freedom, profound purpose and exhilarating possibility. It's about architecting a life that not only looks good on paper or on the 'Gram but feels even more incredible when no one's watching, a life that's rich in joy and authentic fulfilment.

The time for more isn't vaguely "someday". It's not "when things finally calm down". It's certainly not "when you feel perfectly ready" (spoiler: that moment rarely arrives).

The time for more is NOW.

More freedom. More joy. More fulfilment. More impact. This is your moment to decisively break free from the shackles of money worries and begin wholeheartedly funding the dreams that make your heart sing. This is your invitation to step fully into the powerful, prosperous version of yourself you've always intuitively known was possible.

The *More Money, More Life* philosophy isn't just a concept – it's a recalibration. A blueprint for rewriting your money story with clarity, courage, and conscious design. This diagram is more than a visual; it's an invitation – a mirror and a compass – a living framework anchoring your

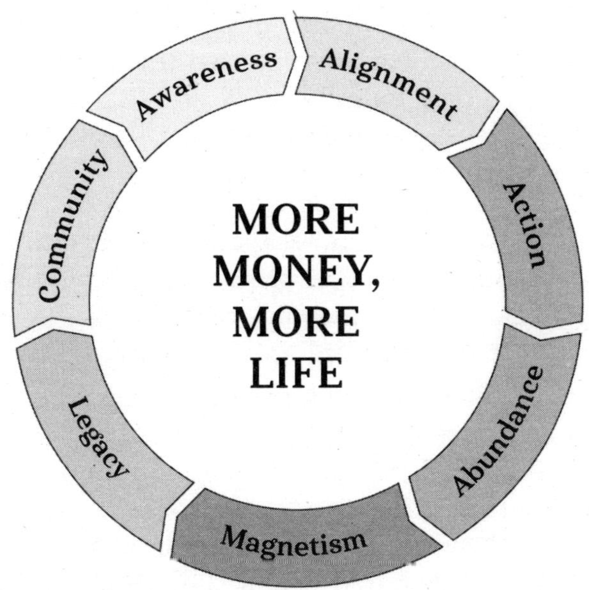

The *More Money, More Life* philosophy

transformation in truth, intention and power. Each pillar – Community, Awareness, Alignment, Action, Abundance, Magnetism and Legacy – marks a dimension of a life lived fully, on purpose. Together, they create the architecture of true wealth: not just what you earn, but how you live, love, give and grow. Every element urges you to rise – to choose expansion over scarcity, vision over fear, authenticity over approval. It calls you to move beyond survival, into a relationship with money grounded in your values, your calling and your joy. This framework bridges everything you've unearthed – old beliefs, inherited patterns, subconscious narratives – and transforms that awareness into empowered, creative action. *More Money, More Life* means living richly in every sense: unlocking your dreams. Nurturing the relationships that sustain you. Building a legacy that reflects who you truly are. This diagram guides you back to your own inner compass. Your story was never meant to be defined by numbers – but by meaning, freedom and fulfilment, written on your own terms. The time for more – more vision, more joy, more life – is now.

Rewrite your story

Journaling is one of the most potent and accessible tools you have for rewriting your personal money story. Think of it as creating a safe, judgement-free sanctuary where you can gently unravel your thoughts, unearth deeply buried beliefs and give your emotions the space and freedom they need to flow. When you put pen to paper, you're doing more than just writing; you're holding up a mirror to your mind. You're granting yourself permission to slow down and self-reflect, to explore with curiosity and to connect with the parts of yourself that are often overshadowed by the beautiful chaos of daily life.

This isn't about crafting perfect sentences or weaving a narrative that needs to make sense to anyone else. This is purely for you. It's a practice rooted in radical honesty, compassionate curiosity and joyful discovery. It's about uncovering the beliefs you didn't even realize you were carrying, lovingly challenging the ones that no longer serve your highest good and intentionally planting the seeds for new, empowering ones that will help you flourish.

When it comes to your money story, journaling is especially transformative. Why? Because money is never just about the maths; it's profoundly emotional, deeply psychological and intensely personal. Your financial reality is so often a direct reflection of your inner landscape: your beliefs about what's possible for you, your relationship with yourself, your sense of worth and the boundaries you set. This is your gentle invitation to dive deeper. So, grab your journal, a comforting cup of tea (or coffee, or wine. No judgement here!), and let's begin this enlightening exploration.

Your reflection prompts

Take a quiet moment to reflect on your own money story using these prompts. Write without any filters, without a shred of worry about "getting it right". Simply allow your thoughts and feelings to flow onto the page.

What are your earliest memories of money? Were they charged with positivity, negativity or perhaps a confusing mix? Think back to the very first time money made an impression on you. Was it spoken about openly and calmly in your family, or was it a topic shrouded in tension or silence? Did it feel like a tool for creating possibilities and joy, or did it register as a source of stress and limitation?

How did your parents or primary caregivers handle their finances? What explicit lessons or implicit beliefs did you absorb from watching them? As children, we're like sponges, absorbing everything around us, often unconsciously. Reflect on the financial dynamics you witnessed growing up. Were your parents natural savers or joyful spenders? Did they approach money decisions as a united team, or did financial discussions often lead to arguments? What unspoken rules, habits or underlying anxieties about money might you have picked up from their example?

When you think about money in this moment, what emotions surface most strongly? Is it fear, excitement, guilt, hope, anxiety or something else entirely? Close your eyes for a moment and take a deep, calming breath. Imagine holding a sum of money in your hands, perhaps your ideal monthly income. What's your immediate, gut-level reaction? A thrill of excitement? A knot of anxiety? A pang of guilt? These emotions are vital clues, like breadcrumbs leading you toward the core beliefs and stories that are currently shaping your financial reality.

What would it truly feel like to live a life without financial stress, where money is a source of ease and empowerment? Vividly picture a life where money flows to you freely and joyfully. Imagine your bills paid with ease, your savings growing steadily and the exhilarating freedom to say "YES!" to the experiences, opportunities and contributions that genuinely light you up from the inside. How would that version of you feel on a daily basis? Confident? Expansive? Generous? Grateful? Peaceful? Hold onto that feeling. Let this feeling become your North Star, guiding you forward.

What are you genuinely grateful for in your financial life right now? Now, bring your focus back to the present with a lens of appreciation. Acknowledge and list at least three specific things money currently provides for you that you are thankful for. It could be the roof over your head, the food in your fridge, the ability to buy coffee for a friend, the internet connection that allows you to learn something powerful, or a past financial lesson that made you stronger. No matter how big or small, connect with the feeling of gratitude for the support and opportunities money already brings to your life today.

These prompts are far more than just questions; they're potent keys to reclaiming your personal power. The stories and emotions you uncover here might surprise you. Some may feel heavy or uncomfortable, while others might trigger an illuminating "Aha!" moment. Whatever emerges, greet it with compassion and honour it as your truth. The more you explore your inner world in this way, the more clarity you'll gain about where you've been and, more importantly, the incredible places you're capable of going.

Journaling isn't about finding all the answers in a single session. It's a process, a practice and an ever-unfolding journey of self-discovery. Each time you return to these prompts, or simply to your journal, you'll likely peel back another layer of understanding, bringing you ever closer to consciously and powerfully rewriting your money story in a way that aligns with your authentic values, your most cherished dreams and the vibrant, abundant life you're ready to create.

So, let the pen flow. Scribble, doodle, rant, dream. Get it all out. Once your pen stops, or you feel a natural pause, simply sit with what you've uncovered for a few moments. There's no need to immediately analyse, judge or "fix" anything. Let your insights breathe and settle. Perhaps revisit your notes tomorrow or in a few days with fresh eyes. The very act of bringing these subconscious stories and feelings into the light of your awareness is profoundly transformative in itself. This isn't a one-time assignment; consider it the beginning of an enriching, ongoing conversation with your soul. Trust the process and trust yourself.

This is just the courageous first step on your journey to financial empowerment. In the next chapter, we'll dive deeper into the fascinating psychology of wealth, exploring the common patterns, limiting beliefs and subconscious stories that can shape your financial reality. Together, we'll uncover practical tools and mindset shifts to help you create a life of genuine abundance, entirely on your terms.

Your new money story isn't just waiting to be written; it's demanding to be forged. Let's seize the pen and begin.

CHAPTER 2
THE PSYCHOLOGY OF MONEY

For so many of us, money feels like an enigma. A complex cocktail of stress, excitement, mystery and even guilt. It's a fundamental part of our daily lives, yet it's something few of us feel we truly understand, even as we relentlessly pursue it, hoping it will unlock new beginnings and brighter futures. Many believe money is merely a game of numbers, spreadsheets and equations. A straightforward balancing act of income versus outgoings. But that, my friend, is only scratching the surface.

In this chapter, drawing inspiration from profound works like Morgan Housel's *The Psychology of Money*, we're going to journey beyond the balance sheets. We'll uncover the potent, often hidden, psychological forces that are shaping your financial decisions. More importantly, you'll discover how to consciously reshape these forces so they align powerfully with the vibrant, fulfilling life you dream of creating.

We all operate with our own unique financial DNA. Yes, you read that right! Your financial DNA is as distinct as your fingerprint, intricately shaped by your upbringing, your environment, the messages you absorbed growing up and your personal life experiences. It's the fundamental reason why two individuals with identical earnings and bank balances can make vastly different financial choices, leading to dramatically different life outcomes. It's why some people seem to effortlessly win at the "money game", while so many others feel perpetually stuck or behind.

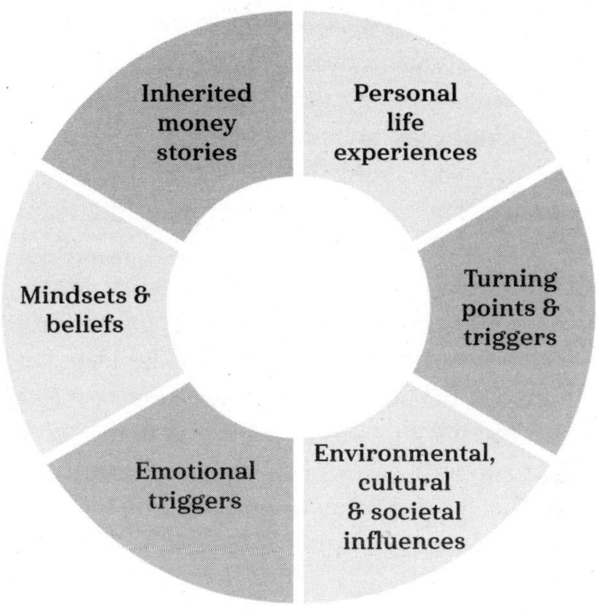

Your financial DNA

Because the truth is that money is so much more than numbers on a screen. It's deeply personal. It's a mindset. It's a complex web of behaviours, deeply ingrained beliefs and the powerful stories you've carried, often unconsciously, for years. Money is intricately woven into the very fabric of human nature, tangled up with our ego, our pride, our deepest fears and even our capacity for love and generosity. It's not just what you know about money that shapes your financial situation, it's how you behave with it. And this is where the real transformation lies. Your behaviour around money isn't simply about willpower; it's driven by your subconscious programming, your emotional triggers and the habitual ways you respond to financial situations. Knowing all the "rules" of finance means little if your underlying beliefs and emotional patterns are secretly sabotaging your efforts. True financial empowerment comes from understanding these behavioural drivers and learning to consciously choose actions that align with your goals, rather than being trapped by old, unhelpful programming.

Think of money as an extraordinary mirror, one that reflects not just your bank balance, but the very essence of who you are. The values you hold dear, the fears you're grappling with and the narratives you've absorbed about your worth and capabilities throughout your life. Imagine standing before a mirror that reveals the unseen, reflecting back not just your physical form, but the intricate landscape of your thoughts, beliefs and emotions. That's precisely how money operates. It's a powerful mirror to your inner world, your relationship with abundance and your deeply ingrained stories about what wealth means and whether you deserve it.

So, if your prevailing inner voice whispers that money is scarce, impossibly hard to earn and always slips through your fingers, that's the financial reality your "mirror" will likely reflect. Conversely, when you cultivate a core belief that money is a tool for freedom, impact and joyful expansion, when you genuinely embrace abundance and your inherent worthiness to receive and create wealth, money begins to flow toward you with greater ease and intention. Money itself doesn't possess a personality; it simply, and accurately, mirrors back the energy and the stories you project onto it. It's these internal narratives that dictate your external financial reality.

Our emotions are powerful drivers of our financial outcomes

Our emotions are powerful drivers of our financial outcomes. Unaddressed emotions frequently sabotage our financial well-being. Fear can trap us in survival mode, leading to hoarding resources, chronically undervaluing our skills or avoiding crucial financial decisions. Guilt may cause us to feel undeserving of wealth, making us shrink from opportunities or hesitate to invest in our own growth and joy. Similarly, shame often whispers insidious lies, such as "You're just not good with money", which reinforces patterns of avoidance, secrecy and a scarcity mindset.

Anger, often a response to perceived injustice or frustration, can manifest financially as impulsive "retail therapy" to soothe emotional wounds, or it might fuel aggressive risk-taking as a form of rebellion. It can lead to resentment toward the financial success of others, or bitterness over past mistakes that perpetuates current inaction and blame. And, envy, fuelled by social comparison, can be a toxic financial driver. It might lure you into the "keeping up with the Joneses" trap, resulting in overspending on status symbols you don't need, accumulating debt to project a false image of success, or fostering a persistent sense of inadequacy, regardless of your achievements, simply because others appear to have "more".

When you consciously shift your emotional state toward gratitude, confidence, abundance and even fun and playfulness around money, your entire financial world begins to transform. You find yourself making empowered choices, spotting opportunities where you once saw obstacles, and welcoming wealth not as a struggle, but as a natural, supportive friend.

Consider two people with identical earnings. Person A believes money is an inherent source of stress and anxiety. They're constantly worried about bills, avoid any form of financial planning and feel a pang of guilt every time they spend money on themselves. Their financial life often feels chaotic, reactive and unstable. Person B views money as a powerful tool for creating personal freedom, positive impact and a life aligned with their values. They manage their finances with clear intention, proactively invest in their personal and professional growth, and experience joy in generously sharing their resources. Their financial life is characterized by growing stability, a sense of abundance and deep purpose.

Your financial reality is a dynamic, evolving journey. Expect your financial mindset to be tested and transformed through life's myriad transitions, such as starting out independently, forming partnerships, raising a family, experiencing loss or navigating significant hormonal shifts like perimenopause and menopause. Each stage is a profound opportunity to consciously reassess, realign and redesign your financial outlook to support your new reality. Hormonal changes, for instance, can deeply affect mood, energy and cognition, making perimenopause a critical life stage for enhanced financial self-awareness and proactive security planning. Failing to adapt your financial strategy during these shifts can lead to stress, misalignment and lost potential.

Money isn't a neutral measure of assets; it's a vibrant reflection of your inner world

Money isn't a neutral measure of assets; it's a vibrant reflection of your inner world. By courageously understanding your beliefs, acknowledging your emotions and consciously nurturing this relationship, you unlock the power to reshape your financial reality, creating a life of greater abundance, purpose and genuine fulfilment.

Forget the myth that lasting financial success hinges on complex formulas or the latest apps. Authentic success is born from your mindset. It's about fundamentally reimagining your relationship with money, transforming it from a source of stress into empowerment, from a symbol of limitation into a beacon of possibility, and from an instrument of fear into a catalyst for freedom and joy. Shift your mindset and you don't just change your finances, you transform your entire life. Because how you think and feel about money profoundly dictates how you live. It's time for you to live abundantly.

A quick history lesson

So, we've explored how deeply personal our money psychology is, now let's zoom out and understand the powerful external forces that sculpt this inner landscape – the sweeping historical and global events we collectively live through. These aren't just news headlines, they become part of our financial DNA.

To truly grasp this, let's imagine someone who grew up in the USA during the 1970s. They might have witnessed the stock market delivering thrilling highs, even amid economic anxieties like oil crises and soaring inflation. Between October 1974 and December 1976, the S&P 500 surged nearly 60%. Investors who held their nerve during the turbulence were often handsomely rewarded, fostering an optimistic view of market resilience and potential for growth.

Now, contrast that with someone born in the UK during the 1950s. They likely grew up seeing the FTSE All-Share Index languish through much of the 1970s. High unemployment and widespread economic struggles painted a grim picture, naturally shaping a more cautious approach to financial risks and investments.

These global events cause seismic shifts that ripple through entire economies, and leave an indelible mark on how we think, feel and act when it comes to our finances. They don't just move markets, they shape mindsets, forging the financial character of entire generations.

Take the 2008 financial crash, a defining moment for Millennials. This was a generation raised on the promise that hard work and higher education were the golden tickets, only to step into adulthood and find the rules of the game drastically rewritten. Dream careers vanished overnight. Homeownership, long seen as a cornerstone of stability, suddenly seemed an impossible dream for many. Savings, if any, drained faster than they could be replenished. What should have been a vibrant period of building and expansion turned into an unexpected masterclass in survival. Imagine the collective shockwave, the very ground felt like it crumbled beneath their feet. And from that rubble, a new financial psychology began to emerge.

For Millennials, the Great Recession of 2008–2009 was more than a crisis; it became a crash course in resilience and adaptability. Faced with a stark lack of traditional opportunities, they didn't just wait; they rewrote the rulebook. They embraced side hustles, dived into gig work, and fuelled a surge in entrepreneurship, forging a new kind of financial independence built on agility, creativity and resourcefulness. It wasn't just about earning money, it was about reclaiming a sense of control and agency. The gig economy exploded. Platforms like Airbnb, Etsy and Uber weren't merely conveniences; for many, they were lifelines, demonstrating that income generation was no longer solely tethered to a traditional 9-to-5. Yet, even as this generation innovated, their relationship with money carried a thread of caution, a healthy scepticism. They learned, by necessity, to prioritize security and flexibility, a mindset that continues to influence their financial decisions. For many, the traditional aspiration of homeownership was thoughtfully replaced with a desire for freedom and a richness of experiences over an accumulation of material possessions. Wealth began to be redefined as less about sheer accumulation and more about crafting a life filled with meaning, balance and the flexibility to live on your own terms.

This isn't just a Millennial story, though. It's a universal truth. Our money psychology evolves in tandem with the ever-changing world around us. Consider the more recent COVID-19 pandemic. Much like the 2008 crash, it fundamentally reshaped our collective understanding of stability and security. And it certainly carved deep lessons into my own life. The pandemic hit just as I was navigating the raw, beautiful intensity of early motherhood for the second time. I returned to a demanding job only six months after my daughter Ophelia was born. It was a whirlwind, a genuine blessing and a curse. A blessing because, unlike so many who faced job losses, I had a job, and the shift to remote working meant I witnessed precious moments of Ophelia's first year, an experience starkly different from my first maternity leave where my eldest was in nursery five days a week. But it was also incredibly challenging. The fear of job insecurity during such global uncertainty was immense, and that fear pushed me. While I'm deeply grateful for the crisis management skills I honed while witnessing our company pivot to fully remote in weeks, the reality was that my maternity leave was cut short, replaced by 80-hour work weeks fuelled by adrenaline and caffeine, all while tending to a baby who, it felt like, never slept! The lesson etched into my soul from that period wasn't just about financial survival, but about the true currencies of life. Time, presence and well-being. While working from home, snatching lunchtime cuddles with Ophelia before her nap became sacred moments of connection that I wouldn't have had otherwise. These experiences crystallized my values, highlighting the non-negotiable importance of being present for my children and the driving need to create a life where my work fuelled my soul rather than drained it. It powerfully reinforced that true wealth encompasses far more than a pay cheque; it includes the freedom to cherish what matters most.

Job losses, furloughs and market turbulence during the pandemic reminded us all of life's inherent unpredictability. Yet, it also sparked a wave of financial awareness and intentional change. People saved more, deeply reconsidered their priorities and bravely embraced new ways of investing, earning and living. The pandemic was a global wake-up call, a stark reminder that the status quo can shift in an instant. And in that upheaval, many of us, myself included, found piercing clarity about what we truly value, what we genuinely need and the incredible resilience we're capable of.

This exploration of historical impact isn't just trivia, it's the foundation of understanding why we each think, feel and act so differently when it comes to money. Our unique tapestry of experiences shapes our reality, influencing how we perceive risk, define wealth and recognize opportunity.

But while global events undoubtedly mould our financial psychology, they absolutely do not have to define our future. The past might leave its marks, but those experiences can become powerful signposts on our roadmap to resilience and conscious creation. If you've ever felt overwhelmed by your financial situation, if you've caught yourself thinking, *"I'll never get ahead"*, or *"This is just the way it is for me"*, please remember this: you are not your current circumstances. While events shape your experiences, you're the author of your responses and, ultimately, your choices. This understanding is your power.

The world will always throw curveballs, but you hold the inherent capacity to adapt, learn, grow and thrive. Just as Millennials forged new paths in the wake of the Great Recession, and just as we all navigated the profound uncertainties of the pandemic, you, too, possess the power to rewrite your money story. The key is to pause, reflect with courage and ask yourself:

- What specific experiences, big or small, have most profoundly shaped my current financial beliefs?
- How have these experiences influenced my views on wealth, risk, security and opportunity?
- What invaluable lessons can I extract from my past to build a more empowered, joyful and abundant financial future?

How our financial DNA impacts others

There's another fascinating layer to your financial DNA. It doesn't just impact you, it profoundly influences your relationships, especially with your partner. Money is consistently cited as one of the top stressors in relationships, and when you understand financial DNA, it's easy to see why. When two people, each with their unique financial blueprint shaped by different experiences and beliefs, come together, it can sometimes feel like trying to mix oil and water. The meticulous saver paired with the spontaneous spender. The audacious risk-taker with the play-it-safe planner. The partner dreaming of splurging on a once-in-a-lifetime vacation clashing with the partner focused on bolstering the emergency fund. Think of the arguments that could be lovingly sidestepped if couples truly understood each other's financial programming and triggers! Exploring your partner's financial DNA isn't just about scrutinizing their spending habits; it's about gaining insight into how they see the world, what makes them feel secure, and what their dreams for the future look like. This will open the door to richer communication, deeper empathy, stronger alignment and truly shared financial goals.

Here's a quick tip to get you started on the road to financial cohesion. Begin having regular "money dates" with your partner. Set aside dedicated, relaxed time to talk openly and honestly about your individual and shared goals, fears and dreams around money. Approach these conversations with a spirit of curiosity and a desire for connection, rather than judgement or blame. Aligning your financial decisions with your partner isn't just about managing a joint account, it's about consciously co-creating your future, together.

Your Triple A pathway to abundance

My **Triple A Framework** addresses Awareness, Alignment and Action. This powerful three-step process will ignite your mindset, awaken your potential, align actions with your soul-values and empower you to build the abundant life you desire and deserve. Let's dive in.

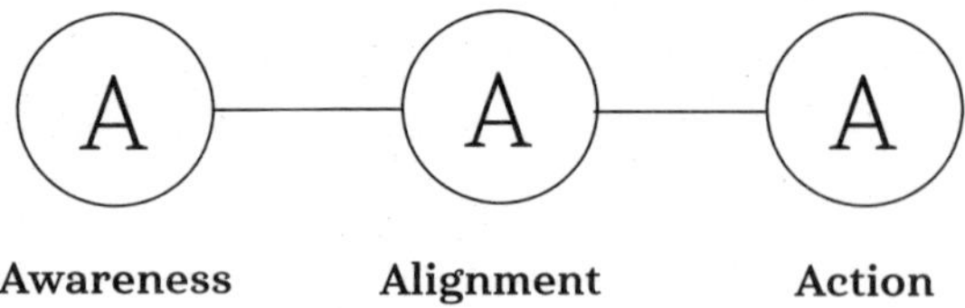

The Triple A Framework

Step 1: Awareness

Awareness is the keystone of all meaningful transformation. It's the sacred starting point of every great journey, because before you can consciously change anything, you first need to illuminate and understand what's currently driving your financial behaviours. This means courageously uncovering those subconscious beliefs about money, the invisible stories running on a loop in the background that subtly shape every single decision you make.

These beliefs didn't materialize overnight, so reshaping them will require patience and intention. But with consistent, compassionate effort and clear intention, you absolutely can unlearn the old patterns that no longer serve your highest good and proactively replace them with new, empowering habits that actively support your financial goals and most cherished dreams.

The next time you hear that sneaky, limiting thought creep into your mind, perhaps a whisper of "*I'll never truly get ahead*" or "*This is all I can realistically afford*", I want you to stop right there! Take a breath and consciously recognize that thought for what it is. A belief, an old story, not an immutable fact. This recognition is a game-changer. Simply acknowledging these thoughts, without judgement, is the first courageous

> The language you use when you speak to yourself directly shapes the actions you take and, consequently, the results you achieve

step toward dismantling their power. Limiting beliefs thrive in the shadows of our minds, so let's shine a brilliant light on them. Name them. Acknowledge their presence, perhaps even thank them for trying to keep you safe in the past, and then consciously choose to replace them with thoughts that expand your sense of possibility.

For example:

- Swap the disempowering thought, "*I'm bad with money*" for the empowering affirmation, "*I'm learning to master my finances and become a confident steward of my resources*".
- Replace the restrictive thought, "*I can't afford this*" with the expansive question, "*How can I create the resources for this if it truly aligns with my goals?*" or "*What steps can I take to make this possible?*"

Your words possess incredible creative power. The language you use when you speak to yourself directly shapes the actions you take and, consequently, the results you achieve. Speak to yourself with the same optimism, patience, understanding and unstoppable belief in your potential that you would offer your dearest friend. Do this because your subconscious mind is always listening, absorbing these messages as truths. When you consistently feed it with encouragement, possibility and self-compassion, you're actively reprogramming it for success and resilience. You're building an internal ally that supports your growth, rather than an inner critic that undermines it. This kindness creates the fertile ground from which all positive change can blossom.

Let me share the inspiring story of Sophie, one of my incredible clients. Her journey beautifully illustrates the profound power of cultivating awareness and courageously reframing limiting beliefs, demonstrating how a shift in mindset is the essential first step in any effective business or financial strategy.

When Sophie first came to me, she carried a belief that so many of us internalize in different ways. The idea that earning beyond a certain figure – for her, it was £100,000 – was a "silly idea". It felt overwhelmingly unattainable, like something reserved for other people, not for someone like her. "We're just a regular family," she'd tell me, her voice tinged with a resignation that masked a deep yearning. "It's just not possible for us to make that kind of money." But Sophie isn't "just regular". She is, in fact, extraordinary. She had already faced and triumphantly conquered significant personal challenges, earned a Masters in Positive Psychology (a testament to her intellect and dedication) and built a remarkable foundation for her business. Yet, her deeply ingrained limiting beliefs were acting like blinkers, preventing her from seeing her own brilliance and immense potential. This conviction that significant financial success was beyond her wasn't just a casual thought, it screamed of an unacknowledged deficit in self-worth. When our self-worth is diminished, we often struggle to recognize our own value and the value of what we offer. This can lead to a cascade of self-sabotaging behaviours like chronic undercharging, hesitating to ask for fair compensation or an unconscious belief that we simply don't deserve substantial success, thereby creating an invisible internal ceiling on our achievements. She was chronically undercharging for her services, sometimes even giving away her valuable time and expertise for free, a classic symptom of this underlying belief.

Sophie, a powerhouse of a coach, ran a vibrant membership club and hosted engaging events. She was unknowingly sitting on a financial goldmine, her vast knowledge, but her mindset was the bottleneck, a silent saboteur holding her back from claiming the explosive success that was already well within her grasp. So, we rolled up our sleeves and got to work, not with complex financial instruments, but with clarity and strategy. We meticulously broke down her potential revenue streams: the realistic subscription fees for her thriving membership club; the inherent value of her events, which we translated into tiered ticket pricing that clearly captured the transformation she offered; and the premium packages she could confidently offer her 1:1 clients, many of whom were already in her pipeline and genuinely eager for deeper, transformative work with her.

When Sophie saw the numbers laid out plainly in front of her, her jaw literally dropped. Making £100,000 a year wasn't just a distant possibility, it was a clear probability based solely on her existing membership club, without even factoring in the full potential of her events and coaching.

But, as we know, real numbers alone don't change lives. Mindset does. So, we then lovingly but firmly tackled Sophie's limiting beliefs head-on. We worked together to consciously shift her internal narrative from the disempowering, "Money is out of reach for someone like me" to the expansive and truthful, "Money is abundant, it's a tool for good, and the more I make, the greater impact I can create in the world."

The critical trigger for Sophie was realizing that by breaking down the numbers, leveraging the existing business she had already built, and executing with a clear strategy, incredible progress was within her grasp. That single, profound mindset shift opened the floodgates to tangible transformation. Within months, Sophie created a budget aligned with her values and ambitious goals. She began consistently saving, something she'd previously deemed impossible, and courageously restructured her offerings, finally pricing her services to reflect their true, immense value.

And the best part? Sophie didn't just break through that £100,000 ceiling; she absolutely smashed it and is now confidently well on her way to achieving her next financial milestone.

Sophie's story isn't an anomaly. It's a powerful reminder of the incredible, life-altering power of awareness. When you dedicate the time to courageously uncover the beliefs that are holding you back, you can begin the transformative work of reframing them. And when you do, you unlock a cascade of new behaviours that naturally align with abundance, opportunity and empowerment. Awareness isn't just the first step, it's the foundational bedrock of everything that follows. It's the master key that unlocks the door to your limitless potential. So, I invite you to pause right now and ask yourself with gentle honesty:

- What core beliefs about money are currently running in the background of my mind?
- Are these beliefs helping me build the life I desire, or are they subtly holding me back?
- How can I begin, today, to flip the script on one of these beliefs to better align with the magnificent life I truly desire and deserve?

This is your starting point. The dawn of your transformation. This is the moment you choose to stop being a passive passenger in your financial journey and courageously start taking the wheel. Because you're capable of so much more than you currently realize. Your potential is genuinely limitless. And it all begins with one powerful, conscious choice. To become aware.

Step 2: Alignment

This is where illuminating clarity meets profound purpose. Alignment is the vibrant heart of true transformation. It's not just about vaguely knowing where you want to go; it's about consciously living in a way that authentically reflects your deepest vision every single day. Let's break this down into actionable, soul-stirring steps.

First begin by crafting your vivid vision of abundance. What does a truly abundant life look, feel, sound, taste and even smell like for you? Close your eyes, breathe deeply and dream expansively. Imagine this life in rich, multi-sensory detail, feeling the emotions that surface as you step into this vibrant reality. Perhaps it's waking in a dream home filled with light and joy, the freedom to explore the world with loved ones creating indelible memories, or the profound satisfaction of building a business or career that leaves a positive legacy and secures your independence. Your vision must be exquisitely personal, resonating with your authentic self, not societal ideals. It should ignite excitement, align with your deepest values and serve as your guiding compass. Seize a moment now, or schedule dedicated time, to capture your vision in writing. Be detailed, be daring and let your imagination fully express itself.

Next, anchor your vision firmly by connecting it to your core values, the essential principles that direct your life. Identify these through the following **Values Compass Exercise**. Begin by brainstorming 20–30 value words (such as security, creativity, learning, community) without overthinking. Then streamline this list to prioritize your top ten current values. From there, refine it to your three to five most fundamental core values – those that are non-negotiable for your soul. The crucial final stage is to define what each core value means to you in action. Articulate how each must be expressed in your ideal abundant life, thereby shaping your financial choices, career path and daily habits to ensure you live in complete alignment.

When I personally did this exercise after a 20-year career in banking, I had a profound realization. My top two core values were "freedom" and "impact". For too long, I had been operating within a system that, while providing security, often felt confining. A space where the unspoken rule was to "bring your best (corporate-aligned) self to work", which sometimes meant leaving parts of my authentic self at the door. The emotional toll of this misalignment was a subtle but persistent feeling of being caged, a yearning for something more expansive. Recognizing "freedom" as a core value wasn't just an intellectual exercise; it was an emotional unburdening. It validated my deep-seated need for autonomy, for the ability to choose how I spend my time, who I work with and how I express my creativity. Similarly, identifying "impact" as a core value connected me to a profound desire to make a tangible, positive difference in people's lives, beyond just financial transactions. This emotional connection to my values became the fuel for making courageous changes, leaving behind the "golden handcuffs" of a secure but misaligned career to build a life and business that truly resonated with my soul.

Align your daily actions with your vision & values

This is where the magic truly happens: intentionally aligning your daily choices and actions with your magnificent vision and core values. It's not enough to simply dream about the life you want; you have to actively, consciously and joyfully *live it* into existence. Every choice, whether big or small, should be a deliberate step bringing you closer to the future you're so powerfully creating.

Ask yourself constantly: "Is this decision, this action, this commitment supporting my vision and honouring my values, or is it subtly pulling me away from them?"

Focus on intentionality. From how you allocate your money to how you invest your precious time, every aspect of your life should reflect the extraordinary life you're intentionally building. With this vision clear, continually ask yourself: "What structures, habits and offerings can I build or refine that directly support this vision and are fuelled by my core values?" This proactive questioning ensures you're not just drifting, but consciously architecting your desired reality.

Let me share Lisa's story. Lisa, one of my amazing clients, was caught in a frustrating cycle of unaligned actions. She dreamed of running a thriving creative agency that allowed her to do meaningful work and spend more quality time with her family. However, her daily reality told a starkly different story. She was chronically overworking, significantly underpricing her valuable services and struggling to secure a consistent pipeline of paying clients. The truth was, many of the clients she was working with simply didn't align with her deeper values, largely because she didn't yet fully believe she deserved better or that her ideal clients even existed.

We started by meticulously crafting her compelling vision. Lisa pictured herself confidently running a successful agency that partnered exclusively with values-driven, inspiring brands. She saw herself working fewer, more focused hours, and earning significantly more, allowing her to be truly present and engaged with her children.

Once her vision was crystal clear and deeply felt, we began the empowering work of aligning her actions. She took decisive action, courageously doubling her rates to reflect her true expertise and immense value, she then laser-focused her marketing on attracting clients perfectly aligned with her core values. Simultaneously, she strategically outsourced lower-value, time-consuming tasks, thereby freeing her precious time and energy for high-impact, revenue-generating projects and vital client relationships. Critically, she also established clear, healthy boundaries, intentionally carving out dedicated, uninterrupted family time each week.

Alongside these operational shifts, she crucially focused on building her authentic personal brand (see Chapter 6). This wasn't about crafting a persona, but about powerfully articulating her unique value proposition, now deeply rooted in her vision and values. She began consistently showing up online, sharing insightful content that genuinely resonated with her ideal clients. By networking strategically with other aligned professionals, she confidently positioned herself as an expert and thought leader in her specific niche, allowing this authentic visibility to magnetize the right opportunities.

Her results? Within six short months, Lisa's agency revenue doubled, and her work–life balance improved dramatically. She wasn't just chasing her vision anymore; she was joyfully living it. And this, my friends, is an example of true wealth. It's never just about the numbers in your bank account. True wealth encompasses and enriches every single aspect of your life. Your emotional, intellectual and physical well-being.

Lisa's transformation wasn't magic; it was the direct result of aligning her business actions with a crystal-clear vision rooted in her core values. This authenticity resonated powerfully, attracting ideal clients and opportunities because people are drawn to clarity, conviction and genuine passion.

Alignment is not a one-time event; it's a way of living consistently true to your values. It's the daily, conscious commitment to show up for yourself, to make choices that serve your highest purpose and to courageously embody the magnificent life you're choosing to create. And the most empowering part is that alignment isn't about achieving an impossible standard of perfection. It's about celebrating progress, not perfection. Every small, intentional action you take toward your vision builds incredible momentum, reinforces your belief in what's possible and brings you ever closer to the beautiful, abundant life you've always imagined.

Step 3: Action

Action is the vibrant heartbeat of momentum; it's where intention meets reality. It's not about chasing an elusive state of perfection, it's about embracing consistent, imperfect progress. Action is the sheer power of choosing, one deliberate step at a time, to move ever closer to the magnificent life you've so clearly envisioned. The true magic of the Triple A Framework crystallizes here, because action powerfully reinforces belief. Every intentional move you make strengthens the neural connections in your brain that empower you to think bigger, aim higher and achieve more than you ever thought possible.

This is where your transformation becomes tangible, visible and deeply felt. Your brain isn't a fixed, static entity; it's an ever-evolving, dynamic landscape, constantly being reshaped by your experiences, your thoughts and, most importantly, your actions. Neuroplasticity is the incredible, scientifically proven ability of your brain to rewire itself, proving that every conscious decision you make, every new, empowering habit you build, is literally creating a stronger, more capable and more confident version of you. Think of it like carving a new path through a dense forest. At first, the trail is rough, unfamiliar and overgrown with old doubts. But the more you consciously choose to walk that new path, the clearer and wider it becomes. Your intentional actions are literally strengthening the neural pathways that shape your new reality.

Science backs this up. In 1949, neuropsychologist Donald Hebb introduced the revolutionary principle of Hebbian learning, often summarized as: "Neurons that fire together, wire together." The more you repeat a specific thought, engage in a particular behaviour or reinforce a certain belief, the stronger the neural connection associated with it becomes. Your brain learns and adapts through repetition, so every intentional, values-aligned action you take is diligently laying down the robust foundation for your future success and abundance. Cognitive Behavioural Therapy (CBT) echoes this profound truth; it irrefutably proves that by consciously shifting your thought patterns, you directly reshape your actions, creating a powerful, positive feedback loop of continuous growth and change.

When you habitually tell yourself, "I'll never make enough money" or "I'm just not good with finances", your brain accepts these statements as immutable truths, unconsciously filtering every decision and opportunity through that limiting belief. It can tragically become a self-fulfilling prophecy. But, when you courageously interrupt that old pattern and instead ask yourself empowering questions like, "How can I creatively generate more income?" or "What's one small step I can take today to improve my financial well-being?", you ignite a brand-new neural pathway. One that actively seeks solutions, opportunities and growth instead of passively reinforcing limitations. Your brain, your incredible ally, starts scanning your environment for possibilities, connecting disparate dots and revealing innovative options you might not have even considered before.

This is the transformative power of intentional reframing and conscious action. It's not just about fleeting positive thinking; it's about actively training your mind to seek and expect abundance instead of defaulting to scarcity. And every single time you take action based on that new, empowering belief, whether it's sending that bold email to a potential client, investing in a course that expands your skills or confidently negotiating a better deal, you strengthen that neural pathway, making it progressively easier and more natural to choose growth over stagnation in the future.

After having my first baby in 2017, like so many new mothers, I felt a profound desire to live a different kind of life, one with more flexibility and purpose. Driven by this desire, I took a leap and set up my coaching business as a side hustle. Alongside this new venture, I started an Instagram account sharing my journey and insights. After realizing that building a traditional coaching business still largely required me to trade precious time for money (an incredibly scarce resource with a demanding full-time job and a young baby), I then pivoted and channelled my skill set into creating children's books. While I didn't make mega-bucks from this particular endeavour, it was brilliant, creative fun. I learned so much along the way simply by getting stuck in, taking imperfect action and figuring things out. Crucially, I learned how to generate income and the skills of marketing my very first product. It was exciting, it connected me to so many wonderful people and it proved to me that I could create something from nothing.

Harness the power of small wins

Big dreams are built on the foundation of consistent small wins. To create unstoppable momentum, break your audacious goals into tangible, achievable, bite-sized steps. For instance, if you want to save £1,000, begin with a clear plan to save £50 this week. If you dream of launching your first product, start by outlining your core idea or creating a basic prototype. Looking to boost your income? Initial research into opportunities, followed by direct action like pitching a new client, confidently asking for a well-deserved raise, or launching that side project are your first steps. Every milestone reached, no matter how small, brings you closer to your grand vision, powerfully proving your capability. Remember, every single win, without exception, deserves to be acknowledged and celebrated.

Celebration isn't just about momentary joy; it's a vital component in building and sustaining momentum. Consciously acknowledging your progress sends a clear, positive message to your brain: "This is working. I'm on the right track. Keep going!" Success isn't meant to be a relentless grind; it's an exciting game you get to play, and you make the rules, so make it fun! Every time you reach a new milestone, intentionally level up your reward. Treat yourself to something meaningful, celebrate with supportive friends or invest in something that fuels your next inspired step.

Remember, success loves company, and your transformative journey isn't meant to be a solo mission. Genuine transformation flourishes within a supportive, uplifting community. Actively surround yourself with people who will not only celebrate your wins with you but challenge you to expand your thinking, offer loving accountability and fiercely champion your potential when self-doubt arises. This might involve seeking mentors for their experienced guidance, working with a coach to dismantle limiting beliefs and clarify your strategy, or joining (or even creating) a vibrant community of peers who provide consistent encouragement and celebrate your progress. Ultimately, success is a team sport, and the right support system is a powerful catalyst on your path.

Recognize the triggers that can derail your inspired action

Even with the best intentions and a solid plan, we all face triggers. Those sneaky subconscious forces that can derail our progress if we're not mindful of them. Triggers are specific moments, emotions or situations that can pull us back into reactive, often unhelpful, behaviours, frequently at odds with our financial goals. They aren't inherently bad; in fact, they're valuable signals, shining a bright light on where our emotions, habits and money intersect.

Recognizing these personal triggers is a superpower. When you learn to pause, reflect and engage with them intentionally rather than reactively, you reclaim your control and your power. Think back to times in your life when your money decisions were driven more by intense emotion than clear strategy. What happened? What was the outcome? Cultivating awareness of these moments allows you to reframe them in the future, consciously shifting from impulsive reactions to intentional, values-aligned choices.

Three common triggers include:

1. **Life transitions:** Significant life events like marriage, divorce, redundancy, retirement or becoming a parent can cause seismic shifts in our financial priorities and emotional states. Without conscious awareness, powerful emotions can easily drive impulsive and potentially detrimental decisions.
2. **Emotional states:** Intense feelings such as fear, stress, loneliness, boredom and even extreme excitement or euphoria can cloud our judgement. Think of "retail therapy" after a particularly tough day, or making risky investments fuelled by an overconfident, euphoric state.
3. **Social pressure:** The relentless comparison culture often amplified on social media, or well-meaning friends urging you to "treat yourself" (when it's not aligned with your goals), can subtly nudge you into making choices that are misaligned with your financial vision and values.

Awareness of your personal triggers is genuinely life-changing. It empowers you to pause, take a breath, reflect and then choose intentionally. With every conscious, values-aligned decision, you take back control, ensuring that every action you take is purposefully building the magnificent future you're so clearly envisioning.

The Triple A Framework is your roadmap through profound transformation – becoming aware of limiting beliefs, aligning actions with your core values, and taking inspired, intentional steps. This journey isn't about striving for impossible perfection, but about embracing a dynamic process for lasting, joyful change.

Holistic wealth

We're often taught that wealth is merely a number, a clinical calculation of assets. But true, deeply fulfilling wealth, the kind that infuses life with richness and meaning, transcends mere money. It's a vibrant state of being, an encompassing abundance. What good is a burgeoning bank account if your mind is exhausted, your body depleted, your relationships strained or your soul disconnected? True wealth is gloriously multidimensional, a deep knowing that you have enough. In heart, mind, body and spirit.

This holistic wealth encompasses:

- **Emotional wealth**: The precious freedom from financial stress, fostering a profound ease, supportive relationships and the quiet confidence that your worth isn't tied to a bank statement. *Foster emotional well-being with a daily gratitude practice, noting things you're thankful for to cultivate joy.*
- **Intellectual wealth**: An unwavering commitment to lifelong learning and growth, not just in skills but in wisdom and perspective, turning challenges into opportunities. *Invest*

in your intellectual expansion through inspiring courses, expansive books or challenging communities

- **Physical wealth:** The boundless energy and radiant vitality to engage with life purposefully, honouring your body as the vessel for your ambitions. *Champion your physical health with non-negotiable self-care, like regular exercise, quality sleep and wholesome nutrition, so your body powerfully supports your ambitions.*
- **Spiritual wealth:** A grounding connection to something greater, a guiding purpose that transforms money into meaning and success into lasting significance, ensuring your existence contributes positively. *Nurture your spiritual well-being with daily stillness or reflection – through meditation or time spent in nature – to stay anchored to your deeper purpose and values.*

When these interconnected forms of wealth harmonize, money becomes a powerful conduit for creating, contributing and elevating life. Operating from this wholeness, financial success feels like a natural, joyful outcome. Wealth, in its truest sense, is who you are and how you live. A conscious, joyful alignment of every action and thought with the vibrant, abundant life you're actively creating.

Money mirror exercise

Transformation begins with a single, courageous step. Perhaps reframing a limiting belief, setting a small financial goal or compassionately acknowledging an emotional trigger around money. It takes patience, but every action reinforces the possibility of change. You don't need all the answers today; transformation is built moment by moment, conscious choice by conscious choice, carving a new path to the magnificent life you've envisioned.

The following **Money Mirror Exercise** will help you uncover your unique stories, identify patterns and unlock your vast potential. By integrating the Triple A Framework here, you'll gain profound clarity, empowerment and a practical roadmap for your ongoing transformation. Here's how you do it:

Reflect on your financial history

Truly understanding your relationship with money begins by exploring its origins. Gently reflect on your early money memories. Were your first recollections concerning money generally positive, associated with joy and security, or did they carry undertones of stress, conflict or scarcity within your household? Consider the spoken and unspoken beliefs you inherited from your family, community or cultural upbringing. Were you taught that money was an empowering tool, or did it feel more like a burden or something unattainable for "people like you"? Think about your most defining personal financial milestones so far. How did you feel earning your first significant pay cheque, taking on debt like a mortgage, making a large purchase or navigating a financial setback?

- **Pro tip:** As you unearth these memories and beliefs, capture them without immediate judgement. The goal isn't to criticize your past, but to compassionately understand its influence on your present. A quick voice note or some unfiltered journaling can be incredibly revealing at this stage.

Uncover your current money mindset

Once you've gently explored your history, it's time to compassionately examine the here and now. Uncover the core beliefs and prevalent emotions driving your current financial decisions. Consider your self-perception and worthiness in relation to money. Do you genuinely feel confident, capable and deserving of financial abundance, or do feelings of anxiety, inadequacy or unworthiness often surface? Identify your emotional triggers. What emotions typically arise when you discuss or think and make decisions about finances? Is it joy and possibility, or more often guilt, fear and overwhelm? How do these feelings shape your subsequent actions or inactions? Finally, honestly assess your prevailing mindset patterns: are your thoughts generally rooted in abundance and sufficiency, or do you find yourself more often focusing on scarcity and limitations?

- **Pro tip:** Start consciously noticing your everyday language around money. Actively replace disempowering phrases like "I can't afford this" with empowering, solution-oriented questions like "How can I make this possible if it's truly important to me?" Your words significantly shape your reality.

Align your financial habits with your vision

With a clearer understanding of your financial history and current mindset, you can now consciously align your actions with your vision for an abundant life. Examine your spending patterns and intentionality – are your purchases generally intentional and value-aligned, or do you often spend impulsively or emotionally? Are you mindfully investing in experiences and items that genuinely bring joy and contribute to your well-being? Evaluate your saving and investing habits. Do you have a consistent, automated savings habit or a clear, purposeful investment plan? If not, what internal or external factors might be holding you back?

And what is your debt management approach? Are you actively working toward financial freedom with a clear plan, or do you feel overwhelmed or avoidant regarding your debts?

- **Pro tip:** Commit to tracking your spending diligently for one full month. Gaining clear awareness of exactly where your money is going is an essential first step toward more intentional and empowered financial management. Often, these insights are game-changing!

Identify areas for inspired change

Awareness and alignment are powerful, but it's consistent, inspired action that turns potential into tangible progress and lasting results. This is where your transformation truly takes root. Start by identifying one or two key negative or limiting beliefs about money that you're now ready to rewrite. For example, consciously replace "I'm bad with money" with an empowering affirmation like, "I'm learning to master my finances and I'm becoming increasingly confident and capable." Think about what small, positive and sustainable new habits you can integrate into your routine, starting now. Could it be setting up an automatic savings transfer, dedicating 30 minutes weekly to review financial goals, or reading one article on personal finance?

Finally, define concrete action steps. What's one specific, tangible thing you can do this week to begin aligning your actions more closely with your financial goals and vision of holistic wealth? Break it down into small, achievable tasks.

Consistent micro-actions are the secret to building unstoppable momentum

- **Pro tip:** Don't let the scale of your vision paralyse you into inaction. Choose *one* small, tangible action from your reflections and commit to completing it this week. Consistent micro-actions are the secret to building unstoppable momentum.

You've now held up the Money Mirror and glimpsed the intricate tapestry of your financial story: the beliefs, emotions and patterns that have shaped your journey thus far. This isn't just information, it's illumination. The power here lies not in self-judgement or criticism, but in compassionate understanding and a courageous commitment to conscious, intentional change. Take these reflections and truly sit with them. Allow yourself to feel whatever comes up. Which insights surprised you the most? Which ones feel like a clear and compelling call to action?

Empower yourself by choosing one significant limiting belief you've uncovered during this exercise. Using the reframing techniques we discussed in the "Awareness" section (see page 34), begin the powerful process of rewriting it into an affirmation that resonates with possibility and your inherent worth. Next, select one current action or habit that feels unaligned with your vision. Inspired by our exploration of "Alignment" (see page 38), identify one small, values-driven shift you can make this week to bring that area into greater harmony. This Money Mirror Exercise is your personal catalyst for profound change. Use these invaluable insights to fuel inspired, intentional actions. Keep your journal close at hand; this isn't a one-and-done exercise. Revisit it often, perhaps quarterly or whenever you feel a need for greater clarity. Let it evolve with you as you grow and transform. Celebrate your courage in facing your truths with honesty and compassion. And always remember that every single step you take toward aligning your money with your soul, your values and your vision is a monumental victory.

CHAPTER 3
ABUNDANCE UNLOCKED

There are moments when the weight of financial struggle becomes unbearable. A stress that transcends the bank balances to invade your energy, power and the very identity you've unknowingly assigned to money. I've been there. For me, that moment arrived on a baking hot day at my kitchen table, head in hands, staring at a bank statement confirming we were sinking. It was dire. Mortgage overdue, savings gone, crushed by credit card debt. A reckless builder had vanished with thousands, thrusting me into full-time financial survival mode. The stress was suffocating; every decision fuelled by panic. Money became a relentless frenemy, always slipping away, leaving me trapped in the same scarcity mindset I'd witnessed in my father before his passing and our subsequent family bankruptcy.

In hindsight, that intense struggle was a profound teacher, forging invaluable lessons. The chaos illuminated fundamental truths about my relationship with money, starting with appreciating its flow. The word "currency", from the Latin *currentia*, means "a flowing", reminding us that money is meant to circulate. Mastering this flow begins with conscious accounting. An acute awareness of what enters and leaves your financial sphere. This isn't just about spreadsheets, it's the psychological act of valuing your resources. Tracking your money becomes an observation of your life's energetic currents. This awareness, coupled with deep gratitude for what you have, however small, creates a powerful psychological shift from lack to appreciation, signalling to your subconscious and the world your openness to abundance.

This understanding extends to the law of reciprocity; what you give, you receive. Generosity, whether of time, money or kindness, initiates a potent energetic exchange, cultivating a sustained high vibrational frequency that attracts positivity and opportunity. It doesn't require grand gestures. I recall Mo, a homeless man whose joy and wisdom radiated despite his circumstances. My weekly spare change and our brief chats lifted my spirits through a genuine exchange of human connection. His warmth met my small offering, creating a reciprocal uplift. This taught me that giving, even modestly, reinforces your own sense of abundance, shifting your focus from what you lack to what you can offer. This internal shift signals you operate from a place of "enough" to share, opening channels to receive more.

Money isn't just numbers on a statement, it's a tangible manifestation of your patterns, beliefs and the silent judgements you've made about your worth and possibilities. Without consciously rewriting your money story, you risk reliving the same challenging chapters. Many of us operate from a deep-seated belief in scarcity, perhaps absorbed from witnessing parental struggles or internalizing phrases like "Money doesn't grow on trees".

This scarcity mindset fuels the belief that wealth is an exclusive club, demanding relentless work and sacrifice for even a sliver of freedom. I understand the overwhelming powerlessness of being broke, how choices seem to evaporate and energy drains under the constant weight of worry. This sustained "fight or flight" mode depletes physical energy, clouds judgement and stifles the creativity essential for building wealth. But abundance doesn't have to be such an arduous climb. Money is pure energy, and it responds to three key elements: Awareness, Alignment and Action (see pages 34–47).

So, consider this. What if your current financial circumstances aren't random? What if they directly reflect your deepest beliefs about your worthiness to receive abundance? Could your bank statement simply be a mirror to what you truly believe you deserve? Money, as an energetic force, responds powerfully when your vision is clear, your beliefs are aligned and your actions are decisive. Mastering this trio won't just alter your financial status, it will transform your entire approach to life.

When I first left my corporate role, fear had me in a chokehold. I froze, hesitated and got lost in endless over-planning, waiting for a "perfect moment", which I learned is a dangerous illusion. I mistakenly believed my financial breakthrough would just happen. Newsflash! Clarity isn't born from passive waiting; it emerges from movement, from taking imperfect but consistent action, from unequivocally showing the universe you mean business. So, my friends, we're no longer waiting, we're moving.

It's time to ditch the scarcity mindset for good, step fully into your financial power and create a life brimming with abundance, freedom and joyous flow. The choice, as always, is yours.

The Alignment Code

It's time to shatter the illusion that money is merely a functional tool. This limited view traps many. Instead of treating finances as a constraint, let's wield them as a powerful catalyst for extraordinary change, transforming your resources into the very symphony of your existence. Imagine every financial decision resonating harmoniously with your deepest values, your money actively igniting passions, amplifying talents and magnifying your power to contribute meaningfully. This is the essence of the **Alignment Code**.

This "alchemy" is the magical transformation that occurs when awareness, an energetic understanding of money, aligned values and decisive action are consciously blended. Your awareness of current financial realities and ingrained money beliefs serves as the base metal. Understanding money as responsive, flowing energy provides the transformative heat. Clarified values and heartfelt desires then act as the purifying agent, ensuring authenticity. Finally, consistent, inspired action is the alchemist's hand, shaping and moulding these elements. Together, they transmute mundane money management into the art of crafting a life filled with purpose and resonance.

You hold the inherent power to mould your money into a dynamic force that aligns with your core beliefs, fuels your most ambitious dreams and significantly magnifies your unique contribution. This is your pivotal moment to break free from financial limitations and craft a life that truly, vibrantly sings with purpose and joy. This journey isn't about restrictive budgeting; it's about becoming the masterful conductor of your life's magnificent symphony, where your finances play a beautiful, harmonious part.

Step 1: BRIGHT goals

Forget the old SMART (Specific, Measurable, Actionable, Relevant, Time-bound) goals. Yes, they're practical and meticulously logical, but let's be honest, they lack soul. They speak to the head, but fail to ignite the heart. What you truly need to propel you toward profound transformation are BRIGHT goals. These aren't just objectives, they're declarations. BRIGHT goals are designed to stretch you, to thrill you, to make your heart race with the exhilarating pulse of possibility. BRIGHT goals don't just sit demurely on a vision board collecting dust, they possess an almost gravitational pull, demanding your full presence, your unwavering commitment and your deepest ownership. They dare you to live unapologetically, to courageously pursue what genuinely lights your soul on fire.

The difference between a SMART goal and a BRIGHT goal is the chasm between a tepid wish and a fervent vow. It's the difference between passively stating, "I'd like to save a bit more money this year" and powerfully declaring, "I will have £10,000 in my 'Freedom Fund' investment account by December 31st because I refuse to let another year pass where I am not actively and aggressively building true financial independence and choice". Can you feel the energetic difference? One is a gentle suggestion, the other is an unshakeable commitment etched with passion.

BRIGHT goals are designed to stretch you, to thrill you, to make your heart race with the exhilarating pulse of possibility

Let's break down what makes a goal truly BRIGHT.

Bold: Set goals that catapult you far beyond your current comfort zone. Don't just aim for incremental improvements, dare to envision monumental shifts. Imagine the electrifying rush of obliterating that suffocating mountain of debt, the profound satisfaction of holding the keys to your dream home or the liberating thrill of confidently walking away from a soul-crushing 9-to-5 to build your own empire. Make your goals big. Make them audacious. Make them unequivocally yours. This isn't about what others deem realistic; it's about what ignites your spirit.

Reachable: Every grand, audacious vision becomes attainable when it's deconstructed into clear, manageable and actionable steps. This is where bold vision meets practical strategy. Map out the journey from where you are to where you want to be. Create interim milestones to track your progress and fuel your motivation, preventing overwhelm. The key is to structure your path in such a way that your success feels inevitable, not intimidating. It's about building a staircase to your dreams, one solid step at a time.

Inspiring: Your goals must act as powerful magnets, pulling you forward with an irresistible force, especially when challenges arise. Choose objectives that ignite your spirit, make your pulse quicken with genuine excitement and fill you with a sense of purpose. Let them be a true reflection of your deepest desires and aspirations. When your goals resonate at this core level, every step taken toward them feels less like a chore and more like an exhilarating adventure. They should make you want to leap out of bed in the morning.

Genuine: Anchor your goals firmly in what truly, authentically matters to *you*, not to society, your parents or your peers. These aren't hollow ambitions designed to impress others; they are purpose-driven commitments deeply intertwined with your core values and personal mission. When your goals are soul-deep, when they represent the truest expression of your desires, intrinsic motivation becomes a powerful, self-sustaining force. You're no longer pushing yourself; you're being pulled by a compelling inner vision.

Heartfelt: Infuse your goals with profound personal meaning and emotion. They should tug at your heartstrings, constantly reminding you of your "why". Why you embarked on this journey and why you absolutely must keep going, even when the path gets steep. Connect them to the people you love, the experiences you crave, the impact you want to make. When your goals are charged with this deep emotional current, every action you take becomes not just a task, but a heartfelt celebration of your journey and your becoming.

Transformative: These aren't just financial targets; they're powerful catalysts for your personal evolution. As you pursue your BRIGHT goals, don't just consider the outcomes, notice the empowered version of yourself emerging at every step. Think about the empowered, resilient, resourceful and unstoppable version of yourself that is being forged with each challenge overcome and each milestone achieved. This is more than wealth accumulation; this is your Wealth BE-ing evolution, a profound shift in who you are and how you show up in the world, with money as a supportive tool for that transformation.

Step 2: Fuel your goals with emotion

To achieve big, bold, BRIGHT goals, you need to feel them in your bones, in every fibre of your being. The secret ingredient here is **Emotional Resonance.** Your brain, marvellous as it is, is wired to respond far more powerfully to feelings than to cold, hard logic. When a goal genuinely excites you, when it makes your heart sing, it activates your brain's reward centres (like the nucleus accumbens), flooding you with dopamine. This neurochemical response makes the process of working toward your goal feel like a win, even before you achieve the final outcome. This intrinsic motivation is far more sustainable than relying on willpower alone.

Visualize your success with vivid intensity, every single day. Close your eyes and immerse yourself in the feeling of triumph. Feel the elation of hitting that ambitious savings goal, the pride of launching your dream business, the peace of financial security. See it, taste it, breathe it in. Engage all your senses. The more detailed and emotionally charged your visualization, the more effectively you program your subconscious mind to align your thoughts, actions and habits with your desired reality. Your subconscious will begin to actively seek out opportunities and solutions that lead you toward your vision.

Pair your goals with powerful affirmations. These are not fluffy phrases, they're potent declarations of your intended reality. Speak them aloud with conviction and emotion. Turn them into daily rituals, perhaps upon waking or before sleeping. Emotionally commit to them, don't just recite them intellectually. Each goal becomes a powerful vehicle for transformation, fuelling new strengths, deeper confidence and more purpose-driven, meaningful life.

Step 3: Master your money mindset

Your mindset is the cornerstone upon which every financial decision and action is built. It's the invisible architect of your financial reality. Therefore, a fundamental step in this journey is to consciously shift your predominant money mindset from one of scarcity and fear to one of abundance and empowerment. Start this crucial process by identifying the limiting money stories that are holding you back – those often subconscious, deeply ingrained scripts that keep you playing small and feeling perpetually constrained.

Once you've identified your limiting beliefs, the crucial next step is to consciously replace them. Commit to actively and consistently instilling these wealth-affirming beliefs until they become your new default:

- Money flows to me easily, consistently and abundantly from multiple sources.
- I am inherently worthy of financial success and profound well-being.
- I make smart, confident and empowered financial decisions that serve my highest good.
- Opportunities to increase my wealth and impact are always available to me.
- I am a capable and resourceful creator of wealth.

Commit to these beliefs daily. Write them down, say them aloud, meditate on them. Let them permeate your consciousness until they become your new default state of mind, naturally guiding your actions, decisions and your perception of what's possible.

Step 4: Intentional budgeting

Your budget is not a straitjacket of restriction; it's your personalized blueprint for financial empowerment. It's the strategic map that ensures your money is diligently working for you, actively funding your dreams and consistently fuelling your grandest vision. Forget the old-paradigm, scarcity-driven restrictive budgeting that feels like a punishment.

This is about intentionality and consciousness, deliberately making every pound and penny count toward your highest priorities and your BRIGHT goals.

Giving every pound a purpose

Zero-Based Budgeting (ZBB) is a wonderfully potent system for taking absolute, intentional control of your finances. The core idea is simple, yet its impact on your financial life can be profound: **Income – Expenses = Zero.** This doesn't mean you're aiming to have no money left at the end of the month – far from it! It means every single pound that comes into your life is given a specific, purposeful job before you even think about spending it. It's about telling your money where to go, instead of wondering where it went.

So, how do you put this empowering approach into action? First, get crystal clear on your total monthly income. This is all the money you earn after taxes (your net income). If your income fluctuates, it's wise to use a conservative average

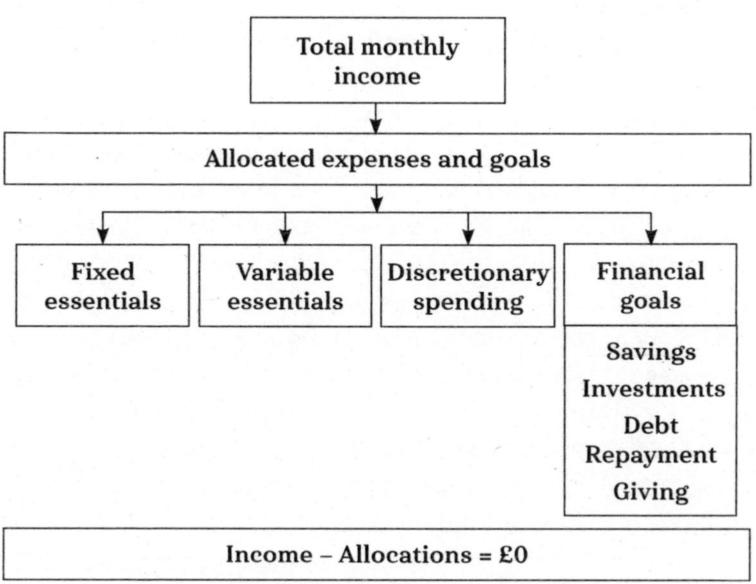

Zero-based budgeting: every pound with a purpose

or your lowest anticipated amount to build your plan on a solid foundation.

Next, and this is where the real insight begins, you'll list ALL your expenses. If you're unsure where your money currently flows, dedicate a month to diligently tracking your spending. It's an eye-opener! Be thorough as you categorize these outgoings. You'll have your fixed essentials, like mortgage or rent, loan payments and insurance, which are typically consistent each month. Then there are variable essentials such as groceries, utilities (which can fluctuate), transportation and childcare. Don't forget discretionary spending for things like eating out, entertainment, hobbies and any non-essential shopping.

> It's about telling your money where to go, instead of wondering where it went

Crucially, a significant portion of your expenses should be allocated to your financial goals. This is where ZBB truly shines, as it forces you to prioritize what you're working toward. This category should include allocations for debt repayment (your minimums, plus any extra you're channelling toward becoming debt-free), building your savings (like your emergency fund, or for specific BRIGHT goals such as a house deposit or that dream travel adventure) and, of course, contributions to your investments for long-term wealth creation. If giving back is one of your core values, make sure to allocate funds for charitable contributions here too.

Once you have your income and a comprehensive list of expenses and financial goals, it's time to **assign every pound a job**. Go through your income figure and allocate amounts to each of your expense categories until every single pound is assigned. The aim is for your total allocated expenses to perfectly match your total income.

For instance, imagine your net monthly income is £3,000. Your ZBB might look something like this: you allocate

£1,000 to rent, £400 to groceries, £150 to utilities and £100 to transportation. Then, driven by your BRIGHT goals, you direct £500 toward debt reduction, save £300 for your travel fund and invest £200. This leaves £350 for personal spending and fun. Notice how the £3,000 of income is fully accounted for by the £3,000 of allocated expenses and goals, bringing you to that empowering £0 balance.

The journey doesn't end with creating the budget; you then **track and adjust** throughout the month. Monitor your spending against your plan. If you happen to overspend in one area (perhaps a few too many meals out), you'll need to consciously decide to spend less in another category (maybe from your travel fund) to stay on track. This isn't about achieving perfection from day one; it's about fostering continuous awareness, making conscious trade-offs and taking responsibility.

Finally, review and repeat monthly. At the end of each month, take some time to reflect. What worked well? Where were the challenges? Adjust your budget for the upcoming month based on your insights and any changes to your income or priorities.

The true beauty of Zero-Based Budgeting is its power to shift you from being reactive with your money to becoming truly proactive. You decide, in advance, exactly where your money will make the most impact, ensuring your spending is a direct reflection of your BRIGHT goals and deepest values, rather than leaving you wondering where it all vanished at month's end. It's you, in complete control, giving every single pound a powerful purpose.

Mastering your inner spender

Alright, so you're armed with your Zero-Based Budget, ready to give every pound and penny a powerful purpose. That's a massive step toward financial command! Our spending decisions aren't always made by the logical, spreadsheet-loving part of our brain, are they? Often, unseen currents of emotion, ingrained habits and subtle external influences are pulling the strings.

If we truly want to achieve a life where our money aligns with our deepest values and BRIGHT goals, we need to go beyond just tracking numbers. We need to become explorers of our inner financial landscape, understanding the "why" behind our "what". This isn't about deprivation; it's about liberation. We're freeing ourselves from mindless consumption so every act of spending becomes a conscious, joyful vote for the life we choose to live.

We've all heard of "retail therapy", that urge to shop when we're feeling down. But the emotional landscape that drives spending is far richer and more complex than just sadness. What about the urge to click "buy" when boredom strikes, using a purchase as a fleeting distraction from an empty afternoon? Or when stress and anxiety are running high, and that new gadget or outfit feels like a temporary soothing balm?

Even positive emotions can lead us astray. That rush of excitement after a win can easily tip into overspending in celebration, going far beyond a deserved treat. Then there's the subtle but powerful pull of social pressure or FOMO (fear of missing out). Buying things not because we need or even truly want them, but to keep up, to fit in or to project a certain image. And let's not forget spending driven by nostalgia or sentimentality, where an object's emotional tether to the past overrides our present financial wisdom.

Take a moment for some honest self-reflection. When do you find yourself spending impulsively or on things that don't serve your long-term vision? What feelings or situations typically precede these moments? Recognizing your personal triggers is the first powerful step toward disarming them.

We're navigating a world meticulously designed to encourage spending

It's crucial to acknowledge that we're navigating a world meticulously designed to encourage spending. Sophisticated marketing and advertising expertly tap into our deepest needs and insecurities. Creating urgency with "limited time offers", leveraging social proof through testimonials or appealing to our desire for status. This isn't cynicism, it's conscious awareness. Understanding these tactics empowers you to choose, filtering external nudges through your internal compass of values rather than being passively swayed.

So, how do we shift from being reactive spenders to conscious creators of our financial reality? It's by weaving mindful, behavioural strategies into our daily lives. Start by embracing the power of the pause; before any non-essential or impulsive purchase, impose a mandatory "waiting period". Perhaps 24 hours for smaller items, a week for bigger ones. Often, the initial urgency dissolves, granting clarity on whether the purchase truly adds value.

Next, make the **Values Alignment Check** your financial North Star. Before buying, ask with fierce honesty: "Does this align with my core values and BRIGHT goals? Will it meaningfully contribute to my *More Money, More Life* vision?" If not, lovingly reconsider. In a culture relentlessly glorifying "more", courageously define your "enough". This isn't about self-limitation but cultivating contentment and appreciating current abundance, which naturally loosens the grip of chasing fleeting things.

To gain deeper insight, try tracking your feelings around spending. For a week or two, note the emotion or situation prompting discretionary purchases. The emerging patterns offer invaluable clues to your emotional spending habits. Armed with this awareness, create healthy "friction" for unwanted habits. If online impulse shopping is a challenge, make autopilot harder: unsubscribe from tempting marketing emails, delete saved payment information or temporarily remove shopping apps. A little intentional friction can be incredibly effective.

Perhaps most powerfully, learn to redirect emotional spending urges with conscious coping mechanisms. When stress, boredom or loneliness triggers that pull, have a pre-planned, non-spending alternative ready. Feeling stressed? Opt for a brisk walk or five minutes of meditation instead of browsing online stores. Lonely? Connect with an uplifting friend or community. Addressing the root emotion intentionally, rather than with a purchase, is where lasting transformation in spending habits occurs. Mastering your spending isn't about austerity but profound self-awareness and empowerment. It's ensuring your financial resources serve your highest vision, funding a life that is secure, aligned, meaningful and joyful. This is how every pound spent becomes a conscious, powerful vote for the incredible life you're intentionally creating.

Make automation your best friend for effortless and consistent wealth-building. As soon as income hits your account, set up automatic transfers: a portion to savings, extra payments toward debts, and contributions to investments. By automating, you pay yourself and your future first, before daily temptations can derail your plans.

And finally, trim the fat but keep the joy. This isn't about deprivation. Scrutinize your expenses. Are there unused subscriptions or habits draining your wallet without adding real value? Reduce spending that doesn't align with your BRIGHT goals or bring genuine joy. However, do ensure you budget for things truly vital to your well-being and happiness. Wealth isn't built through miserable austerity, but through mindful, joyful intentionality.

Step 5: Debt domination

Debt, especially high-interest consumer debt, can feel like an anchor dragging you down, limiting your choices and draining your financial energy. But it's crucial to understand that debt is not your destiny. It's simply a temporary financial situation, a hurdle that you have the power to overcome on your journey to financial power and freedom. Whether you choose the Snowball Method or the Avalanche Method, the key is to commit to dominating your debt with relentless focus and determination.

Let's break down these two popular and effective strategies:

The Snowball Method

How it works:

1. List all your debts (credit cards, store cards, personal loans, excluding your mortgage for this exercise unless it's a specific BRIGHT goal to pay it off early) from the smallest balance to the largest, regardless of the interest rate.
2. Make the minimum required payment on all debts except for the smallest one.
3. Throw every extra penny you can find in your intentional budget (Step 4) at that smallest debt. Attack it with ferocity!
4. Once the smallest debt is completely paid off, celebrate this win! It's a huge motivator.
5. Now, take the money you were paying on that now-eliminated smallest debt (its minimum payment PLUS all the extra you were throwing at it) and add it to the minimum payment of the next smallest debt on your list.
6. Repeat this process. As each debt is paid off, the amount of money you "roll over" (like a snowball getting bigger as it rolls downhill) to the next debt grows larger, allowing you to pay off subsequent debts faster and faster.

The Snowball Method offers a powerful motivational advantage. By focusing on eliminating smaller debts first, you achieve quick wins that provide a significant psychological boost. This rapid, visible progress keeps you engaged and committed, building crucial momentum and fostering the belief that becoming debt-free is truly attainable. This approach is particularly effective for individuals who thrive on immediate results and need that initial motivational kickstart to stay on track, especially if they've previously struggled with adhering to debt repayment plans and require consistent positive reinforcement.

The Avalanche Method

How it works:

1. List all your debts, but this time order them from the highest interest rate to the lowest interest rate, regardless of the balance.
2. Make the minimum required payment on all debts except for the one with the highest interest rate.
3. Channel every extra penny you can from your budget toward the debt with the highest interest rate.
4. Once that high-interest debt is paid off, take all the money you were applying to it (its minimum payment plus the extra) and add it to the minimum payment of the debt with the next highest interest rate.
5. Continue this process until all your non-mortgage debts are eliminated.

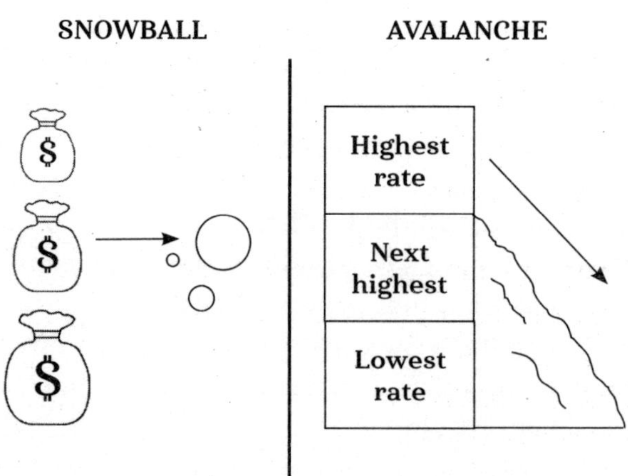

Debt Domination Methods: Snowball vs. Avalanche

If the sheer logic of numbers and maximizing your financial efficiency truly lights your fire, the Avalanche Method might just be your most powerful ally in this debt-domination game. From a purely mathematical standpoint, this strategy is engineered to save you the most money on interest payments over the long run. By strategically zeroing in on and aggressively tackling your most expensive debt first – the one charging you the highest interest rate – you systematically slash the overall amount you'll ultimately pay back to lenders. More of your hard-earned money stays where it belongs – with you!

This path, however, calls for a particular kind of resolve and focus. It's an incredibly potent choice for those of you who are highly disciplined, find deep satisfaction in that logical efficiency, and possess the focus to stay the course, even if that exhilarating first "win" of completely clearing an entire debt takes a little longer. It's about trusting the process and knowing that every single extra payment you hurl at that high-interest beast is a significant stride toward saving you more in the grand scheme of things, supercharging your journey to freedom.

Choosing between the Snowball or Avalanche Method isn't a rigid, all-or-nothing decision. You can absolutely tailor these strategies to your own journey. Perhaps you start with the Snowball to rapidly eliminate a couple of smaller, nagging debts for that initial burst of motivation and momentum. Then, with that victory under your belt, you pivot to the Avalanche Method to tackle the larger, higher-interest debts with maximum financial efficiency. The ultimate goal here is powerful, consistent progress, not absolute perfection in the chosen method. Your freedom is the prize!

Here's a quick-reference table comparing the Snowball and Avalanche methods to help you decide which approach best fits your personality and financial situation:

Feature	Debt Snowball	Debt Avalanche
Payoff	Smallest balance first	Highest interest rate first
Benefits	Quick wins, more motivation	Less immediate satisfaction
Financial Benefits	May pay more interest	Pays less interest overall
Best For	Those needing motivation	Those focused on financial efficiency

Negotiate like a boss

Don't just passively accept the terms of your debt; it's time to become an active architect of your financial freedom. One of your first power moves, especially with credit card debt, is to call your lenders. Yes, pick up the phone! Explain your unwavering commitment to clearing your debt and confidently ask if they can offer you a lower interest rate. The worst outcome is a "no", but you'd be surprised how often they're willing to work with you, particularly if you've got a solid history of making payments.

A savvy tactic is to look for 0% APR balance transfer credit card offers. Imagine shifting that soul-crushing high-interest credit card debt to a new card that charges you zero interest for an introductory period, perhaps 12 or even 18 months. This can be a game-changer, allowing you to plough all your payments directly into reducing the principal amount owed, rather than just servicing eye-watering interest. But hear this, my friends, this strategy comes with a crucial caveat. You absolutely must have a rock-solid plan to annihilate that transferred balance before the 0% period ends, because the interest rate can skyrocket afterwards. And always be eagle-eyed for any balance transfer fees that might eat into your savings.

You might also consider debt consolidation. This involves taking out a new loan, perhaps from your bank or a credit union, at a lower interest rate than your existing debts, and using it to pay them all off. You're then left with one single, often more manageable, monthly payment. This can simplify your financial life and save you a bundle on interest, but again, the golden rule is to ensure that the new rate is genuinely lower than what you're currently paying, and always factor in any loan origination fees. For larger specific loans, like student loans or car loans, don't forget to explore refinancing options if you find you can secure a significantly lower interest rate than your current one.

Every single percentage point you save on interest, every pound you redirect from the lenders' pockets back into your own, is a monumental victory. It's more fuel for your mission, more power to accelerate your debt domination and, ultimately, more freedom to fund your most audacious BRIGHT goals.

Your BRIGHT path to wealth

This journey to financial abundance and alignment is an active one. To help you get started and stay on track, here's a model to draft your own BRIGHT goals and a checklist of key actions. Take some time with a journal or a blank document and work through these prompts for each significant financial aspiration you have.

The core desire: What do I want to achieve financially? (e.g., "Be debt-free", "Buy a home", "Start my own business", "Travel the world for a year", "Build a $X emergency fund").

1 **B – BOLD:** How can I make this goal truly exciting and a little bit scary (in a good way)? What's the audacious version of this?
2 **R – REACHABLE:** What are three to five key milestones or steps to get there? What's the first, most immediate step I can take in the next seven days?
3 **I – INSPIRING:** Why does this goal light me up? What will achieving it allow me to DO, BE or HAVE that I deeply desire? How will it feel?

4 **G – GENUINE:** Is this my goal, or am I pursuing it for someone else or for societal approval? How does it align with my core values (e.g., freedom, security, creativity, contribution)?
5 **H – HEARTFELT:** What's my deep emotional connection to this goal? Who does it impact positively (me, my family, my community)? What's the "why" that will keep me going when things get tough?
6 **T – TRANSFORMATIVE:** Who will I become by pursuing this goal? What new skills, beliefs or strengths will emerge? How will this shape my journey toward true Wealth BE-ing?

Your BRIGHT path to wealth checklist:

- **Set your BRIGHT goals:** Use the model above to define one to three BRIGHT financial goals that stretch you and excite you. Write them down and keep them visible.
- **Fuel your motivation:**
  - Practise daily visualization of achieving your BRIGHT goals. Feel the emotions.
  - Develop and recite powerful affirmations linked to your goals and wealth beliefs.
- **Master your money mindset:**
  - Identify two or three limiting money beliefs you hold.
  - Craft and commit to new wealth-affirming beliefs daily.
- **Budget with intention (Zero-Based Budget):**
  - Calculate your total monthly net income.
  - List and categorize all your monthly expenses (fixed, variable, discretionary).
  - Allocate every pound/dollar of your income to an expense category or financial goal until Income – Expenses = £0.
  - Prioritize allocating funds toward your BRIGHT goals within your budget.
- **Reduce debt (if applicable):**
  - List all your debts.
  - Choose your debt repayment strategy (Snowball or Avalanche).

    - Actively look for ways to reduce interest rates (negotiate, balance transfers).
    - Allocate a specific, aggressive amount to debt repayment in your budget.
- **Automate your finances:**
    - Set up automatic transfers from your checking account to:
        - Savings account(s) for your BRIGHT goals
        - Investment account(s)
        - Extra debt payments
- **Track progress & celebrate milestones:**
    - Schedule regular (e.g., weekly or monthly) check-ins to review your budget and progress toward goals.
    - Acknowledge and celebrate every milestone achieved, no matter how small.
- **Continuous learning & adjustment:**
    - Stay curious and continue learning about personal finance, investing and wealth creation.
    - Be flexible and willing to adjust your plan as your circumstances or goals evolve.

Navigating systemic headwinds

My friends, by now you're feeling that incredible shift within. You've dug deep into your money story, you're aligning your wealth with your soul's purpose and you're beginning to architect your wealth operating system designed for true freedom. The power you've unlocked to shape your personal financial destiny is immense, and that is something to truly celebrate!

Yet, as we build our individual fortresses of abundance, it's also vital to acknowledge the wider ocean we're sailing on. The truth is, the financial playing field isn't always perfectly level. Beyond our personal beliefs and actions, there are broader systemic currents – economic inequalities, ingrained discriminatory practices, and unequal access to financial resources and networks, which can, for some, create significant headwinds. You may have heard me speak of the sobering $1.2 trillion gender wealth gap; this is just one example of how these larger forces can impact individual journeys.

To acknowledge these systemic realities isn't to diminish your personal power or to embrace a narrative of victimhood. Far from it! It's about widening our lens, becoming even more strategically astute, and recognizing that true mastery involves understanding the full terrain. Both our inner landscape and the external environment. This awareness doesn't dilute your agency; it sharpens it, preparing you to navigate with even greater wisdom and resilience.

Think of systemic financial barriers as unseen ocean currents. Unaware of them, you might struggle against their force, wondering why progress feels so difficult despite your best efforts. Deep-rooted economic inequality means opportunities aren't always evenly distributed. Discriminatory practices, based on gender, race or other factors, can manifest as biased lending, unfair pay or limited access to crucial networks. Not everyone begins with the same access to quality financial education or influential connections. Recognizing these currents isn't about assigning blame; it's about equipping yourself with a more complete map to understand the terrain and strategize effectively.

So, how do you navigate these broader systemic headwinds on your *More Money, More Life* journey? First, raise your awareness. Educate yourself about these issues and how they might affect you or your community. Critically, seek financial information, mentors and advisors who understand these wider challenges and offer tailored, culturally sensitive guidance, not a one-size-fits-all approach that ignores systemic realities.

> Remember, where you spend and invest your money is a powerful vote for the world you want

This is where the principles you're mastering in this book become even more potent. Building your Evergreen Wealth

Engine (see pages 95–132), diversifying income through Digital Mastery (see pages 103–8), employing Precision Investing (see pages 108–23), and cultivating your Ikonic personal brand (see pages 141–9) are not just strategies for personal abundance; they're powerful acts of resilience against systemic vulnerabilities. A stronger personal financial foundation insulates you from external shocks and gives you greater agency.

Your community and network are also incredible assets. Intentionally build diverse, supportive connections. Seek out and contribute to communities championing financial empowerment and offering resources, especially for those facing greater systemic barriers. Collective power, through community lending, investment clubs or advocacy groups, can forge opportunities where traditional systems fall short.

As your own *More Money, More Life* takes shape, so does your capacity to influence change. Use your voice and financial choices to advocate for fairness and equity, supporting businesses and organizations actively dismantling systemic barriers. Remember, where you spend and invest your money is a powerful vote for the world you want. And while you may not dismantle centuries of systemic inequality overnight, you can master your personal financial destiny. Focus fiercely on what's within your control: your mindset, skills, financial habits and the systems you build. From this position of personal strength and sovereignty, you're then far better equipped to contribute to the larger, longer-term work of influencing and changing the systems themselves.

The ripple effect: your rise lifts others

Acknowledging systemic barriers doesn't mean surrendering to them. It means becoming a more conscious, strategic and, ultimately, more impactful architect of not only your own life but also of a more equitable world. Every single one of us who breaks through, who builds their own *More Money,*

More Life despite any systemic headwinds, becomes a beacon of possibility. We not only create a more secure future for ourselves and our families but also increase our collective capacity to challenge these systems, to open doors for others and to fund the very initiatives that drive broader change.

This awareness adds another profound layer to your journey. It transforms your personal success into a powerful statement and a stepping stone for wider impact. As you continue to build your abundant life, know that your journey is not just your own; it's part of a larger movement toward a world where everyone has the opportunity to achieve their *More Money, More Life*.

Now is the time. Not tomorrow, not next week, not when things "settle down". Now is the moment to take that bold, decisive action and begin earnestly claiming your financial independence and the abundant life you deserve. Your future self, living with more freedom, choice and peace, will be eternally grateful for the courage and commitment you're demonstrating today. It's not about waiting for the elusive perfect moment; it's about powerfully deciding that now is your time to rise.

CHAPTER 4

MONEY, MEANING & IKONIC WEALTH

This chapter isn't just about money. It's about meaning. It's about the vital connection between your financial world and your soul's purpose. Because let's be honest, too many of us are sleepwalking through our financial lives. Earning, spending, accumulating, maybe even saving, but without a true, animating sense of why. We chase the next promotion, the bigger house, the arbitrary number on a statement, thinking that will be the key to fulfilment. Yet, somehow, the satisfaction remains elusive. That's because money is never just about money. It's intrinsically linked to our sense of self-worth, our connection to purpose and the degree of

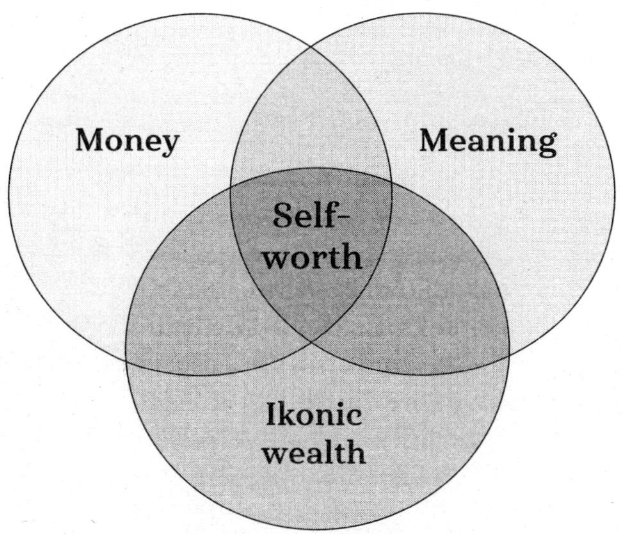

The holy trinity: money, meaning and ikonic wealth

alignment we feel in our lives. True wealth isn't just about looking good on paper; it's about crafting a financial reality that feels as good as it looks, one that resonates with who you truly are.

In this chapter, we're going deep. We'll explore the subtle psychology of self-worth and how it dictates your financial ceiling. We'll uncover the magnetic power that comes from aligning your finances with your non-negotiable core values. And we'll touch upon ensuring the goals you set truly light your soul on fire, building upon the BRIGHT framework we've already discussed (see pages 56–9).

I vividly remember my own turning point. For years, I thought financial success meant hitting certain numbers or acquiring the "right" possessions. But when I hit my personal rock bottom, finding myself unexpectedly broke after being scammed, utterly exhausted and questioning every choice I'd made, I had a stark realization. I hadn't been building true wealth, I'd been desperately seeking external validation. In that moment of crisis, my internal question shifted dramatically. I stopped asking, "How much do I have?" and started asking, "How does my money align with the life I truly want to live and the person I want to be?"

And that, my friends, is when everything began to change. Money transformed from a tool of limitation and stress into a powerful vehicle for expansion. It became a tangible extension of my values, a dynamic force that helped me create, give, connect and grow in ways I hadn't thought possible. I stopped the relentless hustle for external approval and started intentionally aligning my pounds and pence with my purpose. This reveals a crucial truth. Often, we don't have a money problem; we have a meaning problem. We chase financial goals that don't genuinely excite us, grind relentlessly toward milestones that feel hollow upon arrival, and then wonder

Often, we don't have a money problem; we have a meaning problem why we remain stuck in cycles of stress, dissatisfaction and scarcity, regardless of our income.

I saw this play out starkly in one of my former corporate roles. The salary was impressive, but the environment? Soul-crushing. Our team was consistently promised support, resources and recognition that never materialized. We were pulling insane hours, pouring our energy into work that felt fundamentally undervalued and disconnected from any larger sense of purpose. My pay cheque might have looked good, but it was funding a life that felt suffocating, empty and utterly devoid of meaning. It was the epitome of financial success masking a profound poverty of spirit. The issue wasn't the amount of money, it was the gross misalignment. My financial reality, despite the healthy numbers, was completely disconnected from my deeper need for purpose, contribution and authentic expression. When money isn't connected to meaning, it fails to deliver lasting fulfilment. It becomes just a number, unable to fill the void left by work that drains your soul or a lifestyle that doesn't honour your values. This disconnect is a major source of quiet desperation for many high achievers.

Ikonic Wealth

This brings us to the concept of Ikonic Wealth – the energy, the flow, that occurs when your financial vision aligns perfectly with the core of who you truly are. When this happens, money transcends from being a source of stress and becomes a natural conduit for freedom, impact and possibility. It's the underlying reason why some individuals seem to attract wealth and opportunities effortlessly, while others grind endlessly and still feel like they're falling short. This isn't about luck, privilege (though we acknowledge its role) or even sheer relentless hustle; at its heart, it's about alignment.

Money, as we've explored, is fundamentally energy. It's a mirror reflecting your values, your intentions, your beliefs about abundance and deservingness. When your financial choices – how you earn, spend, save, invest and give – resonate deeply with your authentic self, wealth begins to flow to you and through you, not through forceful pursuit, but through conscious embodiment. We've been sold a pervasive cultural narrative of scarcity, one that glorifies the grind, idolizes relentless hustle and suggests that mastering spreadsheets is the key to financial salvation. This story demands constant chasing, pushing, sacrificing. But what if that very narrative, the one promising success through struggle, is actually the biggest barrier to your true wealth? What if the critical issue isn't the volume of your actions, but the depth and clarity of your "why"?

Imagine your transactions not as mere debits and credits, but as intentions made manifest

Imagine your financial ledger not as a cold spreadsheet, but as a vibrant canvas. Imagine your transactions not as mere debits and credits, but as intentions made manifest. Intentions that are consciously aligned with your soul's essence, your core beliefs, the better world you wish to help create. Suddenly, spending isn't just a trail of expenses; it becomes a powerful declaration of your values. Saving isn't deprivation; it's an investment in your future freedom and dreams. Earning isn't just a means to an end; it's an expression of your unique talents and purpose.

We often obsess over the "how" – the tactics, the optimizations, the squeezing out of extra percentage points. Yet, your "why" – your connection to meaning and purpose – is the true engine of sustainable wealth creation. It's the compass guiding you along a financial path that genuinely nourishes your soul, not just your bank account. Your money becomes a tangible vote for the world you desire and the future self you're becoming. Are you casting your votes for a relentless, directionless climb fuelled by external pressure? Or are you voting for a quiet, internal revolution that reshapes everything from the inside out? Are you voting for noise and comparison, or for genuine impact and contribution?

Alignment isn't a luxury, it's your ultimate leverage. It's the profound difference between pushing a heavy boulder uphill and effortlessly riding a powerful current. When your spending proudly proclaims your values and your earning joyfully echoes your purpose, the friction, the stress, the struggle, the feeling of swimming against the tide begin to dissolve. Opportunities arise, collaborations appear and resources flow, often not through desperate pursuit, but through the magnetic pull of your authenticity.

Stop playing a financial game designed by others, bound by rules that don't resonate with your soul. Dare to craft your own game, one where the rules are your values and the goal is a life rich in meaning and money. And here's the beautifully ironic, almost poetic truth. When you prioritize living in alignment with your true self, financial wealth tends to follow, not as the primary obsessive goal, but as the natural, inevitable byproduct.

From getting to giving

A fundamental shift in perspective is required here. Stop asking, primarily, "How much can I get?" And start asking, with genuine curiosity and commitment, "What value can I give? How can I serve?" That single, profound shift changes the entire energetic equation. When your focus moves from extraction to contribution, from getting to giving, you align yourself with the universal principle of flow.

Give more value, deliver exceptional service, serve your community or clients from a place of genuine care. Generosity, in its many forms, creates a powerful ripple effect. It stems from the law of reciprocity, the understanding that energy flows in cycles. When you give freely and joyfully, without attachment to receiving something specific back, you create a positive energetic output. This act floods you with feel-good neurochemicals, endorphins and oxytocin, and shifts your mindset from "not enough" (scarcity) to "more than enough to share" (abundance). This feeling, this vibrational state of abundance and joy, is highly magnetic. Like attracts like. When you consistently operate from this generous, high-vibration space, you attract more opportunities, positive connections and, yes, often more money, because you're signalling to the universe (and your own subconscious) that you're an open channel for abundance to flow through.

To cultivate this mindset, start small. Think about simple acts of kindness or generosity you can incorporate into your week. How can you make someone's day a little brighter? Perhaps create a dedicated account or even just a simple jar labelled "Joyful Giving Fund" or "Abundance Flow Account". Add whatever small amount you can spare regularly. The act itself matters more than the amount. Those tiny, intentional deposits of generosity often yield far more happiness and cultivate a deeper sense of self-worth than a safe full of jewels ever could. It reinforces the truth that your worth is intrinsic, not tied to your net worth. Remember the principle often attributed to Zig Ziglar: "You can have everything in life you want, if you will just help enough other people get what they want." Wealth isn't merely about accumulation, it's about circulation. It's about putting your resources (including money) where they truly matter, allowing them to be a catalyst for positive change, both for others and, consequently, for yourself.

Imagine two highly skilled professionals in the same corporate field. One, let's call her Hermonie, is primarily driven by hitting sales targets and climbing the ladder for status and validation. She achieves conventional success but often feels stressed, competitive and like she's constantly chasing the next external win. The other, Ginny, is driven by a genuine passion for solving client problems and mentoring her team. She focuses on delivering exceptional value and building strong relationships. Ginny also achieves significant financial success, but her journey feels more fulfilling, aligned and less like a relentless grind. She operates from purpose, while Hermonie operates from pressure.

Your financial journey can feel like Ginny's – aligned and fuelled by something far deeper than just the numbers. That's how you cultivate Ikonic Wealth: wealth measured not just by the zeros on a statement, but by the positive impact you create and the meaningful legacy you build.

Embodying your BRIGHT self

Knowing your money story and defining wealth is crucial, but transformation truly ignites when you bridge awareness with aligned action and embodiment. Start living this alignment daily by creating **Sacred Money Rituals** that elevate your relationship with money beyond mere transactions, making financial management feel intentional and empowering. This could involve instituting weekly "money nights" – dedicated time to review your budget, track BRIGHT goal progress, celebrate wins and consciously align spending with your values. Complement this with daily gratitude and visualization; acknowledge the abundance already in your life and feel the emotions of success. Even typically mundane tasks like bill paying can become mindful; approach it by blessing the money leaving, acknowledging the value received and affirming that more is always flowing back to you.

Beyond these rituals, practise **Embodied Wealth**. This isn't "fake it till you make it", but "be it till you become it", acting as if you're already the wealthy, abundant and aligned person you aspire to be. Making decisions from this place of power and alignment, rather than from fear or scarcity, fundamentally shifts your energy and attracts different results. Ask yourself, "How would the version of me who has achieved my BRIGHT goal handle this situation? What decision would they make?" Whether it's investing in a course, negotiating a contract confidently or setting a boundary, making choices from this future, empowered self rewires your brain and accelerates your journey. It's about embodying the feeling and decision-making of your desired state, starting now.

Investing in YOU

Your daily money habits are a direct reflection of your underlying beliefs about your self-worth. If you find yourself constantly undercharging, hesitating to invest in your own growth or habitually overspending to fill an emotional void, it's a clear signal that it's time for a shift. It's time to consciously realign your relationship with money and start making choices that truly honour your immense potential.

Start by charging what you're worth. No more shrinking back or second-guessing, no more discounting your value before you even begin. For those of you running your own businesses or working as freelancers, practise stating your prices clearly and confidently, saying them out loud in the mirror until they roll off your tongue with ease and conviction. Let the energy behind your words fully reflect the incredible value and transformation you provide.

If you're navigating the corporate world, this principle applies just as powerfully when it comes to securing the salary you deserve. Getting paid what you're worth in a traditional job isn't about demanding more just for the sake of it; it's about confidently articulating the value you bring to the organization, rooted in that same deep sense of self-worth. Stop waiting passively for incremental cost-of-living increases or hoping someone magically recognizes your contribution. Instead, take

> Invest powerfully in your growth, not just financially but emotionally, intellectually and spiritually

empowered action. Research industry benchmarks and market rates for your role, experience level and location – knowledge is power. Meticulously document your achievements, quantifying your impact whenever possible. Did you save the company money? Increase efficiency? Lead a successful project? Exceed your targets? Build your case with concrete evidence. Then rehearse the conversation. Role-play asking for the raise or negotiating your salary for a new position. Get comfortable stating your desired figure and calmly, confidently presenting the evidence of your value. Remember, this isn't about being aggressive, it's about owning your contributions and ensuring your compensation reflects the skills, experience and results you deliver. Just like the entrepreneur setting their prices, you're signalling your self-respect and belief in the value you provide within the company structure.

Next, and critically, invest powerfully in your growth, not just financially but emotionally, intellectually and spiritually. This is arguably one of the most crucial pieces of the wealth-building puzzle, often overlooked in conventional financial advice. Choose investments in yourself that stretch you, challenge you and unequivocally call you to rise to your next level. Whether it's enrolling in a high-level mastermind or transformative course that pushes your boundaries, hiring a mentor who sees your potential even when you can't, or embarking on an experience that forces you out of your comfort zone. Make decisions that boldly declare your unwavering belief in your own potential. You're not just "spending" money on these things, you're strategically fuelling your evolution.

Skills are your most valuable, leverageable asset. Over the past decade, I've been obsessed with understanding how real, sustainable wealth is built, way beyond the hype. I've studied psychology, business strategy and the energetics of money, and I've been privileged to interview or research numerous self-made millionaires. These aren't lottery winners or trust fund beneficiaries, they're individuals who built significant wealth through grit, smart decisions, strategic skill development and a long-term vision.

Naturally, I looked for commonalities in their tangible assets – stocks, real estate, businesses. And yes, those were often present later in their journey, but what surprised me was the universal asset they all cultivated before achieving significant financial success. Their own high-value skills. When I say skills, I mean learnable, income-producing capabilities like strategic marketing, persuasive communication (copywriting/sales), effective leadership, negotiation, coding, complex problem-solving, financial literacy (beyond basic budgeting) or public speaking. One seven-figure e-commerce entrepreneur told me, "Mastering digital advertising was the skill that made me more money initially than any stock." A top executive coach shared, "Doubling down on communication and leadership fast-tracked my promotions and enabled me to launch my own firm."

The pattern was undeniable. They didn't get rich then develop skills; they first developed high-leverage skills, applied them relentlessly, and that led to wealth. Why this sequence? Unlike traditional assets, skills don't require significant capital to build. Just your time, energy and commitment. A valuable skill is potent: it allows you to generate income immediately through a job, freelance work or your own business; it significantly increases your resilience against economic shifts; and it can even multiply the returns on other assets because you'll invest smarter, market more effectively or negotiate with greater strength. Indeed, many individuals leveraged specific skills to create substantial income streams from scratch. Consistently, the top wealth-building skills I identified included sales and persuasion, digital marketing, compelling communication, deep financial literacy and effective leadership or team-building.

While traditional assets like stocks and real estate are crucial for long-term passive growth (and most millionaires eventually invest heavily in them), they often come after skills generate the initial capital. If you're starting your wealth journey, your most potent investment isn't a stock tip, it's acquiring and mastering a high-leverage skill. Pick one that resonates and has market demand, go deep in mastering it (6–12 months of focused effort), start applying it to earn income early (don't wait for perfection) and then channel those earnings into traditional assets. That's the less glamorous, often overlooked, foundational path to sustainable wealth. It starts with building you. I know investing in yourself can feel complicated, especially if you carry subconscious blocks around worthiness. For me, it did. I would elaborately invest in my two daughters without a second thought. The best clubs, education, experiences, because I fiercely believe in their potential. Yet, booking that one transformative course I knew would accelerate my own growth would lead to hesitation, procrastination and inventing excuses not to do it.

Why this self-sabotage? Deep down, I'd absorbed the damaging childhood belief that my needs were secondary, my worth contingent on serving others. This pattern of people-pleasing and self-neglect often originates as an early coping mechanism. An attempt to gain love, approval or safety in unpredictable environments. It can forge a deep-seated conviction that investing time, energy or money in oneself is inherently selfish or undeserving. This belief system directly sabotages financial well-being, often leading to an inability to claim fair compensation, a reluctance to invest in personal growth that could boost earning potential, and difficulty setting boundaries crucial for protecting the time and energy needed to build wealth. Ultimately, people-pleasing isn't genuine altruism; it's a survival strategy, a futile attempt to fill an internal void of worthiness that can only truly be healed from within.

The turning point came with the powerful realization that these patterns, born of past survival needs, were now actively hindering my thriving. The narrative of unworthiness wasn't my truth to own any longer. I began to understand that setting healthy boundaries isn't selfish, it's essential self-preservation. Prioritizing my own growth isn't indulgent, it's a fundamental requirement for showing up fully in the world. Investing in myself wasn't taking away from others, rather it was about building a stronger, more aligned, more capable version of me, better equipped to serve and contribute. And when I finally made the conscious choice to invest in myself – my skills, my well-being, my mindset – everything shifted. My confidence soared, my leadership abilities blossomed and I became a more present, joyful and empowered mother and entrepreneur. Because when you invest in your own evolution, you're not just building a better life for yourself; you're creating a powerful legacy of resilience, strength and possibility for everyone around you.

Stop waiting. Stop hesitating. Make the courageous choice to prioritize your own evolution as fiercely as you prioritize others. You're worthy of growth. You're worthy of investment. And trust me, when you rise, you lift everyone around you.

Self-worth is your wealth foundation

Your financial reality is fundamentally built upon your deep-seated sense of self-worth. It transcends mere numbers; it reflects how you perceive yourself and what you truly believe you deserve. If, deep down, you harbour feelings of unworthiness regarding wealth and success, you'll, often unconsciously, find subtle (and sometimes not-so-subtle) ways to sabotage your own progress. You might overspend to fill an inner void, chronically undercharge because you fear rejection or judgement, or consistently play small because stepping into your full, radiant power feels inherently terrifying.

Let's talk specifically about undercharging for a moment, because this was a major stumbling block for me. I used to feel a physical knot in my stomach every time I had to state my prices or discuss fees for my services. I'd agonize over whether it was "too much", question if I was "really worth it", and often convince myself that lowering my rates would somehow make me more approachable or relatable. In reality, it just left me feeling undervalued, overworked and resentful. Deep down, the fear was that if I charged my true worth, potential clients would question my value or, worse, walk away.

The empowering truth is that charging what you're worth is a profound act of self-respect

But undervaluing yourself doesn't make you more likable or relatable; it simply depletes your energy. It sends a subconscious signal to the world that you lack confidence in your own value, and people invariably pick up on that energy. The empowering truth is that charging what you're worth is a profound act of self-respect. It signals clearly to others (and to yourself) that you stand firmly behind the transformation and value you provide.

So, how do you begin to break this detrimental cycle? You consciously realign your mindset around worthiness. Start by actively training your brain to internalize your inherent value through daily affirmations. Use powerful, present-tense statements like: "I am inherently worthy of wealth and abundance. I confidently charge for the immense value I deliver. My unique skills and expertise are valuable and in high demand." Repeat them consistently, feeling their truth, until they become your deeply held reality. Equally important is to curate your circle. Be incredibly intentional about who occupies your inner sphere. Surround yourself with positive, supportive individuals who genuinely see your brilliance, celebrate your successes and courageously challenge you to step into your fullest potential, while distancing yourself from those who drain your energy or reinforce scarcity thinking.

Unleash this profound inner work directly into your financial decisions. When the moment of choice arrives, whether it's pricing your genius, investing in your growth or setting your financial boundaries, command your choices from a place of confidence, expansive abundance and undeniable self-worth. Reject the old default of fear, lack or people-pleasing. No more justifying your rates or apologizing for your audacious ambitions; own them. Command them. With grace. With conviction. Because this is your financial sovereignty.

It's fundamentally important to cultivate self-worth, because when you truly honour your inherent worth, the universe tends to respond in kind. Opportunities that align with your value begin to flow more easily. Clients respect your boundaries and prices. You shift from a state of constantly hustling for scraps to creating and attracting from a place of centred abundance and resolute self-assurance. What do you do with these results? You leverage them. Use your increased confidence to negotiate better deals. Use the aligned opportunities to build momentum. Use the respect you gain to set healthier boundaries, protecting your time and energy. Use the abundance you've generated to reinvest in your growth, give generously and design a life that reflects your true value.

Stand firm in your values. Own your worth. And just you watch as your financial reality begins to beautifully mirror your empowered mindset.

Tools for aligning your actions with your core values

So we've explored the power of alignment, how harmonizing your money, meaning and self-worth creates Ikonic Wealth. Now, let's translate that into tangible, powerful actions you can take to embody this alignment in your daily life.

First, connect with your inner compass to truly align your finances by knowing what genuinely matters most. Deepen the **Values Compass Exercise** we touched upon earlier to create a living manifesto for your life. A potent method is the **Three Whys Technique**: for each of your top three to five core values, ask "Why is this truly important to me?", answer honestly, then repeat "Why?" twice more for that answer. This strips away surface desires to reveal your raw, motivating essence. Further anchor these values by practising **Values in Action**. Instead of just recalling aligned moments, actively relive them in your mind with vivid sensory detail, focusing on how it felt in your body. The more powerful the emotion, the stronger the anchor.

Then, conduct an **Alignment Audit** by journaling honestly; looking at your life today through the lens of your core values, where are your daily choices (spending, time, work, relationships) reflecting them? Where are the gaps? What one or two small adjustments can you make this week to live in greater harmony?

Next, channel your finances into your purpose. Your purpose is your unique declaration of intent and contribution. **Craft your Ikonic Manifesto**: your declaration of your Ikonic purpose, an actionable statement that defines your intent. For instance, it might be: "To empower women entrepreneurs with the financial confidence and strategic tools to build profitable, impactful businesses they love" or, for a corporate leader, "To cultivate a team environment where every individual feels valued and inspired to achieve their full potential".

With your manifesto clear, **Map your Financial Flow**. Think of your finances as an energy river. Outline your primary income sources and major expense categories, then honestly assess how well this current flow supports your Purpose Manifesto and core values. Where is energy being diverted from what truly matters? Finally, design an **Ikonic Allocation Plan**. Consciously dedicate specific portions of your financial resources to goals that reflect your deepest purpose and values. Whether that's investing in new skills, funding passion projects, strategic philanthropy, building a "Freedom Fund" for purpose-driven choices, or saving for experiences that embody what matters to you the most. Make your money an active force that works for your purpose.

Fortify your self-worth

Abundance flows most readily to those who believe themselves truly worthy of receiving it. To cultivate this deep self-worth, begin by actively deconstructing any limiting beliefs that whisper you're "not smart enough", "don't deserve wealth", or that "it's selfish to invest in yourself". Confront these narratives with an **Evidence Audit**. For each limiting belief, diligently seek out and document concrete life experiences that disprove it. Past successes, skills mastered, challenges overcome and positive feedback received. Your mind may cling to old stories, but persistent focus on this counter-evidence will weaken their hold.

Don't just acknowledge your strengths, own and amplify your unique value. Create a **Brilliance Portfolio**, even if it's a personal document to start. List your key skills, significant accomplishments, glowing client feedback and impactful projects. Regularly revisit and expand this portfolio, using it as a foundation to confidently showcase your unique value proposition in all your work and communications.

Recognize that you cannot pour from an empty cup. Strategic self-investment and regular **Recharge Rituals** are not indulgences but essential maintenance for a high-achieving life. Identify and schedule non-negotiable activities that refill your energy and reinforce your sense of worth and purpose. Simultaneously, pinpoint strategic investments in yourself – courses, coaching, vital health practices or enriching experiences – that directly fuel your growth and purpose, and ensure these are prioritized within your financial planning. Make investing in your own evolution a non-negotiable.

And then, integrate potent affirmations into the fabric of your daily life to solidify these new beliefs. Make your **Wealth-Affirming Statements** visible. Maybe on sticky notes or as phone reminders. Record yourself saying them, or weave them into your meditation practice. Let declarations like, "My unique skills create incredible value, and I am compensated generously", "I am worthy of investing in myself; my growth benefits everyone" and "I confidently own my strengths and celebrate my successes" become the soundtrack to your rising abundance.

Pretty's transformation

Let's visit my brilliant client Pretty's story through this alignment lens. Pretty, a talented agency owner, felt trapped. Her branding gigs barely paid the bills, she lived with her parents and felt suffocated, unable to understand why money eluded her despite her skills. She loved the creative work but felt a profound lack of deeper meaning and financial traction.

When we worked together, the breakthrough came when she connected with her core values through the **Three Whys Technique**: creativity, contribution and freedom. We then crafted her **Ikonic Manifesto**: "To empower small businesses with impactful visual storytelling that amplifies their positive impact". This brought immediate clarity. She saw how misaligned her current reality was. The low-paying gigs often weren't with businesses making a positive impact, and her financial stress severely limited her freedom. The impulse buys she made were a way to seek fleeting comfort from this misalignment.

This new **awareness** fuelled **alignment** and then **action**.

1 **Values/purpose alignment:** She audited her spending, cutting subscriptions and impulse buys that didn't align with creativity, contribution or freedom.
2 **Purpose allocation:** She intentionally redirected funds: 20% to professional development (enhancing her creative skills), 10% to community support/pro-bono work for a cause she believed in (contribution), and 15% to her "Freedom Fund."
3 **Self-worth/action:** Armed with testimonials as evidence against her "not worthy" belief, she confidently restructured her pricing and actively sought clients whose missions

resonated with her Ikonic Manifesto. She created a portfolio showcasing her impactful work.

The powerful link between meaning and money here is undeniable. By aligning her business (how she earned money) and her spending (how she used money) with her core values and purpose, Pretty didn't just increase her income, she reignited her passion. The confidence gained from honouring her worth allowed her to charge appropriately. Attracting clients whose missions she believed in infused her work with meaning. Building her Freedom Fund gave her a tangible sense of progress toward her value of freedom. Within six months, she tripled her income, moved into her own space and felt deeply fulfilled by her craft. Her finances became the bedrock supporting her purpose, unleashing her potential. This transformation is available to you, too, when you commit to aligning your money with your authentic self.

Your money should be your servant, not your master. In the next chapter, we'll dive into practical strategies to build your **Evergreen Wealth Engine**, a proven system designed to help you sculpt new income streams, automate your finances and forge a relentless path toward lasting financial freedom. We're about to engineer a system that doesn't just fund your dream life; it actively amplifies it. It's time to set the wheels in motion and ignite wealth that defies circumstance.

Let's build an Ikonic life.

CHAPTER 5
BUILD YOUR EVERGREEN WEALTH ENGINE

Take a deep breath. Feel that shift within you? The person who picked up this book is not the same person reading these words now. You've journeyed through the often-unseen landscapes of your personal money story, courageously confronted the shadows of inherited beliefs and ignited a potent, undeniable truth within your soul. That quiet hesitation, the subtle self-doubt you once felt around money and your own potential, is now being replaced by a burgeoning laser focus, a fire in your belly, an unapologetic hunger for a life that radiates not just financial abundance, but profound purpose and meaningful impact. Your life isn't just changing; you're becoming unstoppable.

Each step we've taken together so far has been a crucible, forging a new, empowered relationship with wealth, transforming it from mere currency into the dynamic fuel for your freedom, your most audacious dreams and your lasting legacy. The heavy chains of scarcity thinking lie shattered behind you. Lingering doubt has yielded to illuminating clarity. Money, once perhaps a source of stress, confusion or even shame, is steadily transforming into your trusted ally, a powerful and versatile tool ready to amplify the magnificent, values-driven life you're intentionally creating.

Now, we arrive at a pivotal threshold. This is where your internal revolution meets external reality. Where soul meets strategy. Where your crystal-clear vision ignites tangible, sustainable creation. In this chapter, we move decisively beyond the exhausting, outdated narrative of relentless hustle, the pervasive burnout cycle that tragically traps so many brilliant, ambitious minds. We're not here to simply work harder; we're here to build smarter, to transition from labour to leverage, exploring multiple pathways to build your bridge to wealth and a more fulfilling life. This involves becoming conscious architects of systems that make money work for you: tirelessly, globally and in perfect alignment with your deepest values. As emphasized in the concept of building value through values, it's about integrating purpose into every facet of your business.

Close your eyes for just a moment and truly visualize it. Funding your wildest dreams without a flicker of hesitation. Travelling the world with your loved ones, completely unbound by financial constraints. Giving back generously, with an open heart, to the causes that stir your soul. Waking each morning bathed in the quiet, unshakeable confidence of genuine security. This isn't some far-off, unattainable fantasy. This is the tangible promise, the imminent reality, powered by what I call your Evergreen Wealth Engine.

Financial independence isn't a distant luxury reserved for a chosen few

Think of this engine not as a static collection of assets, but as a dynamic, living, breathing ecosystem meticulously designed for potentially limitless income streams and unbreakable financial independence. It's a robust framework built not on chasing fleeting, high-risk trends, but on enduring, time-tested principles of value creation and intelligent leverage. It's about waking up each day knowing your wealth isn't just stable, but actively growing, consistently thriving and perfectly harmonized with the unique, fulfilling life you're choosing to live.

Your money exists to serve you, not the other way around. Financial independence isn't a distant luxury reserved for a chosen few; it's a strategic and spiritual necessity for living a life of authentic purpose and empowered choice. It's the freedom to say an enthusiastic "yes" to soul-aligned opportunities and an emphatic, guilt-free "no" to obligations that drain your precious energy or dim your brilliant light. It's the unshakeable bedrock upon which you build a life without compromise, a life lived fully on your own terms.

But constructing this powerful engine often requires us to confront our existing foundations, and sometimes they're messier than we'd like to admit. Before we dive into the roadmap, let me share a moment of raw honesty. For years, my own financial life was far from the picture of serene control you might imagine, despite a successful career steeped in the heart of banking. A comfortable salary acted as a deceptive veil, hiding a rather chaotic reality of forgotten subscriptions quietly bleeding cash from my accounts, credit card charges I barely registered making, and a vague, passive hope that, somehow, things would magically sort themselves out. In truth, that ignorance felt safer than the anticipated overwhelm of facing reality. It was a subconscious strategy to avoid the discomfort of accountability, a way of sidestepping the fear that I wasn't truly as "on top of things" as my professional image might suggest. This avoidance, this choosing of perceived safety over clear-eyed reality, is a common trap that keeps so many from stepping into their financial power. It's this very pattern we're about to dismantle as we build your engine, because true financial strength is built on clarity, not illusion.

The catalyst for my own financial reckoning came when I left a long-term corporate role. Standing at that significant life crossroads, I knew with bone-deep certainty that I couldn't carry the old financial baggage – the disorganization, the avoidance, the underlying anxiety – into my new chapter. It was time for an honest, unflinching audit. I carved out a dedicated week to untangle the financial mess I'd allowed to accumulate. It began with an almost archaeological dig for lost corporate pensions. Those ghosts of past opportunities and deferred dreams. Then came the stark, unavoidable truth of my cash flow, every single transaction laid bare. The maxed-out credit card, a silent monument to years of mindless, often emotional, spending demanded urgent attention. And those countless subscriptions, the "great deals" I'd signed up for in fleeting moments of impulse or aspiration, were revealed as digital dead weights, relentlessly draining resources for services I rarely, if ever, used. There were, I discovered, no refunds for financial naivety.

Facing this financial reality wasn't just about confronting the numbers on a page; it was about confronting the deep-seated fear that lay beneath them. The fear of truly seeing how much I'd let slip away through inattention, the uncomfortable feeling of being a fraud despite my professional banking background. For so long, it had felt easier, safer not to look. But finally looking, truly seeing the unvarnished reality, was like stepping into blinding, cleansing sunlight after years spent in a dimly lit room. It was the pivotal moment I began reclaiming genuine control, not just of my finances, but of my agency, my choices and, ultimately, my life.

My most profound realization emerged in the period that followed. Even while earning significantly less than my corporate salary, I began to feel a sense of wealth I'd never known before. It was the wealth of control, the richness of intentionality. Every financial decision became empowered, deliberate. Knowing precisely where my money was going, having a clear plan, experiencing that profound feeling of ownership. That was true prosperity, long before my bank balance began to significantly reflect it. This journey to financial mastery isn't just about spreadsheets and sophisticated strategies; it's fundamentally about reclaiming your power. Too many brilliant, ambitious women remain unknowingly trapped, trading their precious energy and time for money, stuck in a soul-crushing pay-cheque-to-pay-cheque cycle, or chained to businesses that demand their constant, exhausting presence. This, I assure you, is not your destiny. True wealth is the power to choose. The power to create. The power to live fully, authentically and joyfully, on your own terms.

Imagine, for a moment, that money is no object. What incredible choices immediately open up for you? Launching that passion project that sets your soul on fire? Exploring distant lands and immersing yourself in new cultures? Deepening connections with your family, creating precious, lasting memories? Generously funding causes that ignite your spirit and make a tangible difference in the world? Financial mastery isn't about hoarding wealth; it's about unlocking a universe of possibility. It's the ultimate currency of freedom. We're moving decisively beyond the outdated, exhausting hustle culture. We embrace smart, sustainable and scalable wealth creation. Visionary women everywhere are courageously building financial empires without sacrificing their well-being, launching impactful global online businesses, strategically investing for long-term growth and creating sophisticated automated income streams. They are mastering what I call **Evergreen Earnings**.

Now, let's be refreshingly realistic. There's no magic "passive income" button you can press. Every income stream, especially in its inception, requires initial input, strategic thinking and intelligent, focused effort. But Evergreen Earnings are fundamentally different from trading hours for money. They represent the valuable assets you build, the intellectual property, the systems, the investments. The significant value you create once, which then continues to generate income for you over time, often with minimal ongoing effort. It's the work that pays you perpetually, long after the initial creation is complete.

This requires **Strategic Leverage**. This means using your resources, your time, your knowledge, your network, your capital in the most intelligent and impactful way to achieve outsized results. In finance, as in life, constantly reacting to daily noise, chasing short-term thrills or spreading your

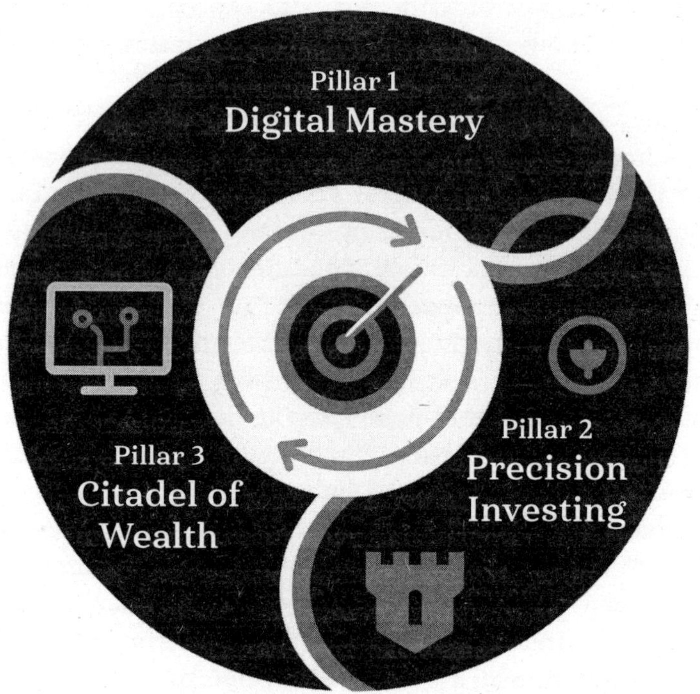

The Evergreen Wealth Engine

energy too thin leads to exhaustion and mediocrity, not empires. Instead, we build systems. Reliable, proven and increasingly self-sustaining systems. That's the very core of your Evergreen Wealth Engine. An income-generating powerhouse meticulously designed to thrive and grow, regardless of fleeting market whispers or turbulent economic storms. This engine doesn't just fund lifestyles; it buys freedom. True, unadulterated freedom from the daily grind, from the linear trap of trading hours for dollars, from the gnawing, underlying anxiety of perpetual survival mode. It liberates your time, grants you the potential for location independence, and builds a

> This engine doesn't just fund lifestyles; it buys freedom

profound sense of security that is untethered to a specific job or a ticking clock. It undeniably builds unshakable confidence. It strategically leverages your greatest assets, your unique knowledge, your valuable network, your intelligent investments, to construct lasting, potentially generational, wealth. It is, in essence, an automated machine diligently working for your prosperity, even when you're sleeping, travelling or focusing on other passions.

This kind of empowerment is crucial, especially when we consider the unique financial landscape many women navigate. Sobering statistics, like those from McKinsey & Company highlighting the disproportionate job losses and career setbacks women often face during economic downturns, underscore a stark reality. Financial mastery and independent wealth creation aren't just aspirational goals; for many women, they're vital lifelines – the key to navigating uncertainty, building unshakeable security and ensuring their voices and contributions are valued in a world that can often feel precarious.

I remember when those statistics felt like a direct reflection of my own terrifying reality. Before I consciously started building my own Evergreen Wealth Engine, I was the classic solopreneur on the brink of burnout. Juggling every conceivable task, desperately chasing every lead, perpetually feeling like I was one cancelled client away from financial disaster. I was living the frustrating paradox of the overworked business owner still trapped in a pay-cheque-to-pay-cheque existence. The weight of being the main provider in our family felt immense and, at times, unbearable. This wasn't just about the money; it was about the constant, underlying fear that stole my peace and creativity, a fear that many women, whether entrepreneurs or employees striving for security, can relate to.

Then there was Maria, one of my gifted clients, a brilliant brand designer pouring her heart and soul into her freelance work. Yet, she was trapped by a cycle of undercharging and overworking, the pressure almost crushing as a single mother who had previously faced an unexpected job loss. For Maria, and for me in those earlier days, one unforeseen event – a client leaving, an illness, a family emergency – could unravel everything. Fear was a constant, unwelcome companion.

The shift, the profound unlocking of potential, happens when you finally crack the code to leveraged, systemic wealth creation. It often requires seeking mentorship from those who've successfully navigated the path, embracing new systems and technologies, and consciously, courageously crossing the threshold from earning linearly (your income directly tied to your hours) to earning with leverage (your income generated by assets and systems). My own journey was filled with messy experiments, a fair share of "failed" attempts (which I now see as valuable lessons) and more than a few sleepless nights spent refining strategies. But the first time revenue arrived in my bank account from a digital product, literally while I slept, it felt like I'd unlocked a cheat code to reality. It was a tangible, exhilarating glimpse of genuine freedom. Building these engines isn't about instant gratification; it demands discipline, strategic thinking and the courage to break the deeply ingrained, socially conditioned habit of trading your precious time directly for money.

My path involved intellectual leverage – a fancy name for strategically packaging my expertise and experience into scalable digital courses and programmes, effectively decoupling my income from the hours I worked. I learned to leverage online platforms to automate marketing, sales and delivery, enabling me to reach a global audience far beyond what my 1:1 capacity could ever allow. This wasn't about replacing personal connection but about creating systems that could deliver value to many, while freeing me to engage more deeply where my personal touch was most impactful.

Maria, with dedicated guidance and a newfound belief in her value, courageously transformed her business model too. She began creating high-value, sellable design templates and launched a subscription service offering ongoing support, decisively breaking free from the exhausting hourly billing trap. The change for both of us, and for so many others who embark on this path, wasn't just financial; it was a fundamental, identity-level shift from scrambling in fear and uncertainty to operating from a place of empowered purpose and calm confidence. That is the profound promise of the Evergreen Wealth Engine; you'll reclaim not just your finances, but the very fabric of your life.

The Evergreen Wealth Engine

Building this engine isn't about succumbing to complex financial wizardry and you don't need an MBA to understand it. It's about strategic simplicity, grounded in three powerful, interconnected pillars. This is the architecture of enduring wealth, meticulously designed for generating true Evergreen Earnings and creating value that lasts. Crucially, at the heart of this engine, particularly for Pillar 1, is the authentic expression of your personal brand. In a world saturated with information, trust is the rarest and most valuable currency. Your unique voice, your story, your clearly articulated values are what build genuine connection and make your offerings resonate. Before people invest in your products or services, they must first invest their trust in you.

Pillar 1: Your steps to Digital Mastery

So, the idea of Digital Mastery has ignited a spark within you. The thought of transforming your unique knowledge, your hard-won experience and your passions into valuable digital assets that generate income and impact truly resonates. And it absolutely should! This is where your intellectual capital takes flight, forming a powerful cornerstone of your Evergreen Wealth Engine.

But perhaps a little voice whispers, "Where on Earth do I even begin? It all sounds so big!" My friends, every digital empire, every thriving online community, every transformative course started with a single, courageous step. We're not aiming for an instantly perfected, all-singing, all-dancing digital product. Instead, we're focusing on smart, intentional first moves that build momentum and illuminate your path. Let's break down those crucial initial steps to get you moving from an inspiring idea to a tangible digital reality.

1. Is your idea a diamond in the rough?

You have a brilliant idea for an online course, a vibrant community or a genuinely helpful guide. That's fantastic! But before you pour your precious time and energy into its creation, let's ensure it's not just a great idea to you, but a valuable solution that others will eagerly invest in. This validation process is your secret weapon against wasted effort.

First, become a **Problem Detective**. Your most potent digital offerings will often solve a specific, pressing problem or fulfil a deeply felt desire for a particular group of people. Tune into the online spaces where your ideal audience gathers. Social media groups, forums, niche communities. What questions are they asking? What are their expressed frustrations, their dreams, their aspirations? Listen with intent. Does your idea directly address a pain point or a passion they're already vocalizing? Next, before you even think about building anything substantial, test the waters with a **Minimum Viable Conversation**. Reach out to a few individuals who represent your ideal audience. Share your fledgling idea with them, not as a sales pitch, but as a genuine inquiry. Ask about their current challenges related to your topic. Would a solution like yours be genuinely helpful? What features or outcomes would make it irresistible to them? And critically, would they consider paying for such a solution? These initial conversations are pure gold, offering invaluable insights.

You can also gauge interest before you fully build by creating a soft launch or a simple way to test demand. Perhaps create an early-bird waitlist for your future course, offering a special incentive for the first few to join. Consider running a free taster workshop on a small, compelling part of your topic. See who attends and eagerly absorb their feedback. Another simple yet effective method is to create a survey asking about the biggest struggles your audience faces in your area of expertise. Their responses will not only guide your content but also clearly show you where the real energy and interest lies. Remember, validation isn't about seeking permission; it's about gathering vital intelligence. It ensures you're building something the world actively wants and needs, aligning your efforts with genuine demand right from the very start.

2. Building your tribe on a shoestring

"But I don't have a huge online following!" I hear this so often, and it's a perfectly normal starting point. Let me assure you, building your initial audience, your first true fans, isn't about having a massive marketing budget or becoming an overnight viral sensation. It's rooted in authentic connection and consistently providing genuine value.

Begin by tapping into your warmest connections, but do it authentically. Think about your existing network – friends, family, past colleagues and professional acquaintances. Are any of them, or perhaps people they know, part of your ideal audience? Share what you're exploring with them and ask for their honest feedback on your idea. Then, start to be generously visible where your ideal audience already spends their time. Reach out to the online groups, forums and social media spaces you identified as relevant to your niche. Don't just charge in promoting yourself. Instead, participate genuinely. Answer questions, offer helpful advice from your area of expertise and share insights freely. Allow your passion and knowledge to shine naturally. People are invariably drawn to those who offer value without an immediate expectation of return.

You can also begin to create **breadcrumb content**. You don't need to write a novel or produce a feature-length film to start sharing your value. Think small, potent and easily digestible pieces. A helpful tip shared on social media, a blog post addressing a common question in your field, or a simple downloadable checklist offering a quick win for your audience. These "breadcrumbs" serve to demonstrate your knowledge, attract organic interest and give people a tangible taste of the value you provide. And crucially, when you do get your first few clients, students or community members – even if they're part of a beta test group – make their experience exceptional. Delight them. Over-deliver on your promises. Listen intently to their feedback and make them feel truly seen and valued. These initial champions, when genuinely delighted, become your most powerful and enthusiastic marketers through authentic word-of-mouth. Remember, particularly in these early days, the depth of your connection will often trump the sheer breadth of your reach. A small, engaged tribe who truly knows, likes and trusts you is infinitely more valuable than a vast, indifferent crowd.

The depth of your connection will often trump the sheer breadth of your reach

3. Crafting a simple first offering

The pressure to create something absolutely perfect and utterly comprehensive right out of the gate can be utterly paralysing, stalling even the most brilliant ideas. Let's consciously ditch that notion. Your first digital offering doesn't need to be your life's greatest work. It needs to be a strategic starting point, a way to deliver real, tangible value, learn directly from your audience's engagement and build momentum. Think in terms of a **Minimum Viable Offer**. The simplest, most focused version of your idea that still provides a clear solution or a desirable result for your audience.

What might this look like? Instead of a sprawling ten-module signature course, perhaps you could offer a focused paid workshop or webinar. Could you teach one core concept effectively, or solve one specific, nagging problem for your audience in a 90-minute live online session? This format is quicker to create, often easier to market and provides invaluable immediate interaction and feedback. If you love to write, maybe your first offering is a concise e-book or a premium, in-depth guide. This could be a well-crafted resource that solves a particular problem more comprehensively than your free “breadcrumb” content, showcasing your deeper expertise.

If you have a larger course or community in mind for the future, consider launching a beta programme or a **Founding Members’ Circle**. Offer this initial version to a small, select group at a significantly reduced price. Be transparent with them; they’re your founding members, and their active participation and honest feedback will be invaluable in shaping and refining the final, polished product. This approach reduces the pressure on you to achieve perfection from day one and beautifully co-creates value with your earliest supporters. And don’t forget, you can leverage your existing skills directly. Could your first digital offering be a package of one-on-one consultations or coaching sessions, delivered online, based on the very expertise you’re planning to scale into a course or group programme later? This allows you to earn income and gather testimonials while you fine-tune your more leveraged offering.

The goal of your first simple offering isn’t necessarily to make millions overnight (though that remains a fabulous long-term aspiration!). It’s to make that crucial first digital sale, to get real-world feedback from paying customers, to learn what truly resonates with your market, and to build your own confidence as a digital creator. Each small win you achieve here acts as powerful fuel for the next stage of your Digital Mastery.

This journey into Digital Mastery, my friends, is an exhilarating one, and it begins not with a giant leap, but with these intentional, often imperfect, yet courageous first steps. Each validated idea, each new authentic connection forged, each simple offering successfully delivered, is another vital gear turning smoothly in your Evergreen Wealth Engine. This is how you start to move closer to a life defined by greater freedom, more profound impact and ever-expanding abundance. Take that first step.

Pillar 2: Precision Investing

Up until now, our focus has largely been on mindset, money stories and the active creation of income. Now, we turn to a crucial component of long-term wealth – making your money work for you through investing. For many, the word "investing" can conjure images of complex charts, risky bets or something reserved for the financial elite. Let's demystify it. At its heart, investing is simply allocating your resources (primarily money) in a way that has a high probability of generating more resources or value in the future. It's about moving from solely earning money to also growing money.

Precision Investing is an undeniable pillar of your Evergreen Wealth Engine. It's the thrilling shift from solely earning money to proactively commanding your resources to grow, forging the path to lasting financial independence and funding those BRIGHT goals (see pages 56–9) that set your soul alight. For too many, the very idea of "investing" looms like an impenetrable fortress, guarded by complex jargon and seemingly reserved for an exclusive club of financial wizards. So, my friends, it's time to dismantle that fortress, brick by brick.

> Investing, in its most powerful essence, is an act of profound faith in your future self

Investing, in its most powerful essence, is an act of profound faith in your future self. It's about nurturing the seeds of today's efforts so they blossom into the abundant tomorrow you're so intentionally designing. It's a cornerstone of your *More Money, More Life* existence.

While we'll explore the types of assets you might consider investing in, like index funds, ETFs and individual stocks (see pages 118–20), part of our journey is about laying the absolute foundation. These are your essential first steps, the practical keys to unlock the world of investing with clarity and bold confidence. Remember, every master of their craft was once a nervous beginner, and the most courageous act is often simply starting.

A note on your financial journey: an important disclaimer

This book is designed to be a powerful educational and inspirational guide on your journey to becoming financial empowered. The strategies, stories and frameworks shared, especially within this chapter on investing, are intended for general informational purposes only. My goal is to help you expand your understanding and feel more confident in navigating your financial world.

However, it's crucial to remember that this does not constitute individual financial advice, and the information provided should not be used as the sole basis for making financial decisions. Your financial situation is unique to you. Investing always involves risk; returns are not guaranteed, and it's possible you get back less than you originally invested.

For personalized advice tailored to your specific circumstances, I encourage you to consult a qualified and regulated independent financial advisor. Please also note that in the UK, the Financial Conduct Authority (FCA) does not regulate all aspects of financial planning, including cash flow planning, estate planning, or tax and trust advice.

Consider this your launchpad for discovery, and always pair the inspiration you find here with diligent research and professional advice on your path to building wealth.

Decoding investment accounts

Before your money can embark on its growth adventure, it needs a vehicle, a dedicated space to flourish. Think of investment accounts as sophisticated launchpads for your financial rockets. Each launchpad is engineered for a specific mission, offering distinct advantages, especially concerning how your hard-earned growth is or isn't taxed.

You might be familiar with tax-efficient wrappers like **ISAs (Individual Savings Accounts)** in the UK, which are truly fantastic. But the landscape of accounts is broader, designed to serve various aspects of your wealth-building journey. You'll encounter **General Investment Accounts (GIAs)**, sometimes called taxable brokerage accounts. These are often the most straightforward, offering great flexibility in what and how much you can invest. The trade-off is that significant profits or income generated might be subject to tax, so it's a space where you should remain mindful of your tax landscape as your wealth expands.

Then there are the accounts dedicated to your longer-term vision, especially retirement. Your future self will thank you profusely for paying attention here! Retirement accounts, like **workplace pensions** and **Self-Invested Personal Pensions (SIPPs)** in the UK, or **401(k)s** and **IRAs** in the US, are specifically designed to be your steadfast companions on the journey to a financially sovereign retirement. This is one of the simplest and most tax-efficient ways to begin your investing adventure. Contributions can be made directly from your salary, and many employers offer the fantastic incentive of matching contributions, providing an instant boost to your investment. These plans usually provide a range of investment choices, including diversified funds or target-date funds that cleverly adjust their risk level as you get closer to retirement, making the "set it and forget it" approach incredibly powerful for building long-term wealth. Governments often sweeten the deal with tax advantages, perhaps allowing your contributions to be tax-deductible or letting your investments grow shielded from tax until you decide to draw upon them in your golden years.

The core reason for this variety in accounts usually circles back to tax efficiency and aligning with your specific life goals. Understanding the unique purpose of each type will empower you to select the optimal launchpads for your diverse financial aspirations. If your gaze is fixed on a horizon decades away, such as a rich and fulfilling retirement, a dedicated retirement account is often your most powerful ally. For goals nearer in view, or once you've made the most of your tax-efficient allowances, a GIA can offer the flexibility you need.

Selecting an investment platform

Once you have a sense of the type of account that aligns with your mission, your next quest is to select an investment platform. This is your partner in the process – the company or online service that flings open the doors to the investment markets, enabling you to buy, sell and manage your chosen assets.

With a universe of providers vying for your attention, this choice can feel like navigating a galaxy. But fear not! Let's illuminate the path. You're looking for a platform that not only functions flawlessly but also feels right, a true ally on your journey. Consider how its fee structure impacts your growth; you want transparency and fairness, as these costs are a direct drag on your returns. Explore the range of investments it offers, does it open up the world of funds, ETFs and stocks you're keen to explore as part of your Precision Investing strategy?

Critically, especially as you begin, gauge its ease of use. The platform should feel intuitive and empowering, not intimidating. A clear interface and straightforward processes for finding investments and making transactions are non-negotiable. Many offer excellent mobile apps, allowing you to connect with your growing wealth wherever you are. And be mindful of the research and the educational tools it provides. A commitment to your continuous learning is a hallmark of a great platform, offering guides, articles, and insights to sharpen your financial acumen. Think about the human element. When that inevitable question pops up, or a flicker of uncertainty clouds your path, who will you turn to? This is where you truly investigate their customer support. Are they genuine partners on your journey, ready with accessible, responsive and helpful guidance? You deserve to feel supported, not lost in a maze of automated responses.

And does the platform roll out the welcome mat for everyone, regardless of where you're starting? Look into their minimum investment requirements. You're seeking a space that empowers you to plant your first courageous seeds, even if they're small, just as enthusiastically as it supports those planting orchards. The rise of "fractional shares" is a beautiful testament to this shift, a wonderfully democratizing force that means you can own a piece of even the most renowned companies, truly inviting everyone to begin their wealth-building journey.

Finally – and this, my friends, is the non-negotiable cornerstone real peace of mind – ask is this platform a fortress of security and regulation? Before you entrust your hard-earned resources and future dreams, ensure they are overseen and regulated by the appropriate financial authority in your country (for instance, in the UK, we look for the Financial Conduct Authority – FCA). This isn't just red tape; it's your vital shield, a powerful layer of protection that empowers you to invest with greater confidence, knowing there are rigorous standards and safeguards in place.

Your action step here is to become an explorer. Dedicate a little time to identify two or three platforms that resonate with your initial requirements. Dive into reviews from trusted financial commentators and everyday users, meticulously compare their fee structures and immerse yourself in their online presence. Many even offer demo accounts, a risk-free playground to familiarize yourself with their universe before you commit your precious capital.

For a wonderfully hands-off start, **Robo-Advisors** offer automated, algorithm-driven financial planning. You'll typically answer some questions about your unique financial goals, your comfort with risk and your timeline. Then these intelligent digital platforms will craft and manage a diversified portfolio for you, often using low-cost ETFs or mutual funds. With low minimum investments and fees that are usually lower than traditional human advisors, they can be a good way to get started. While this automated approach is a strong entry point for many, it's always wise to consider how it aligns with your personal comfort level and understanding. If you're ever unsure, a conversation with a qualified financial professional can bring valuable clarity to ensure it's the right fit for your unique *More Money, More Life* vision.

Investigate fees and commission

Let's zoom in on fees, because these silent assassins of wealth can have a colossal impact on your long-term success. Even fractions of a percent, compounded over decades, can mean the difference between a good outcome and an absolutely stellar one. As an empowered investor, becoming a fee detective is one of your most vital roles.

You'll encounter trading fees or commissions, a charge levied each time you buy or sell. While some platforms champion commission-free trading for specific investments, others apply a flat fee or a percentage. If you envisage making frequent trades (though for the long-term wealth builder, less is often more), these can certainly accumulate. Then there are platform or account fees (sometimes called custody fees), which are the platform's charge for safeguarding your investments. This might be a fixed annual sum or, more commonly, a percentage of your portfolio's value. It's crucial to calculate how this will play out for your specific situation.

When you invest in collective vehicles like mutual funds or ETFs, there'll be fund management fees (often referred to as the Ongoing Charges Figure – OCF, or an expense ratio). This is the cost of the professional expertise managing that fund. As we've discussed, the beauty of passively managed index funds and many ETFs often lies in their wonderfully low fees. This charge is typically factored directly into the fund's performance, so while you may not see it as a separate line item, it's there, influencing your returns. Be vigilant too for other potential charges: transfer out fees if you decide to switch platforms, inactivity fees if your account lies dormant, or currency conversion fees when venturing into international investments.

Your mission, should you choose to accept it (and you absolutely should!), is to scrutinize the full fee schedule of any platform you consider. It's usually tucked away, but it's there. Understand every charge. Don't let enticing introductory offers blind you to the standard costs that follow. Your aim is to secure a reputable, robust platform that delivers the service and access you need, transparently and competitively.

Aligned investing

Embarking on an investment journey means embracing the understanding that risk is an inherent part of the adventure. The value of your investments won't always travel in a straight upward line; there will be ebbs and flows, and yes, you could get back less than you initially invested. This truth isn't meant to deter you, but to empower you to make choices that are deeply aligned with your personal circumstances and your unique emotional landscape. This alignment is a core tenet of building your "Citadel of Wealth", ensuring your financial decisions resonate with your values and your capacity for navigating uncertainty.

So, how do you truly tune into your own risk appetite, ensuring your investment choices are a powerful extension of your unique circumstances? It begins by looking honestly at the landscape of your life right now.

First, consider your time horizon. How long will it be before you anticipate needing this money? If your BRIGHT goals – perhaps that vibrant retirement you dream of, or funding your children's university adventures – are nestled comfortably many years, even decades, into the future, you generally have a greater capacity to navigate the market's inevitable ebbs and flows. This longer runway means you can consider investments with higher growth potential, which naturally come with higher risk. However, if your goal is more immediate, say within the next five years, wisdom dictates a more cautious, steady approach.

Now, what if your financial foundations feel a little less like solid rock and more like shifting sand? Perhaps your income stream feels more like a trickle than a confident flow, that emergency fund resembles a shallow puddle rather than a deep, comforting well, or those high-interest debts are still casting a long, unwelcome shadow. When this is your reality, my friend, it's a clear signal for a strategic pivot. Prioritizing capital preservation often becomes not just appropriate, but your most empowering path forward.

What exactly is "capital preservation" you ask? Imagine it as fiercely guarding the wealth you've already worked so hard to create. When your financial ground feels unsteady, your primary mission shifts from an aggressive pursuit of rapid growth to ensuring the core of your money (your capital) remains intact, secure and ready for you. It's like building your financial fortress brick by painstaking brick, making absolutely certain each one is solid before you even think about adding the magnificent towers.

Your mindset is vital when your foundations are still settling, because when that financial cushion is thin, any significant loss from a bolder, riskier investment can be destabilizing. It can set you back, amplify stress and dim your brilliant light. Choosing capital preservation at this stage isn't about "playing small" or resigning yourself to missing out on big opportunities. Far from it! It's an incredibly savvy and intentional strategy. It's about consciously creating the breathing room you need to strengthen those crucial foundations. To build up your emergency savings until they feel like a buffer against life's unpredictable moments, to relentlessly pay down those soul-draining, high-interest debts, and to solidify your income streams until they flow with confidence.

So, let's translate this into tangible action. It might mean you choose to keep more of your readily accessible money in ultra-safe havens. Think certain types of savings accounts where your initial capital is protected, even if the growth isn't making front-page news. If you dip your toes into investing during this phase, you should opt for very low-risk options, designed more to gently outpace inflation than to shoot for the moon. The focus here is on shielding your hard-earned capital from potential decrease.

Ultimately, this approach is about dissolving financial anxiety and meticulously building that solid, secure base. From this empowered position, you can then explore investments with "more zest" and far greater confidence when the time is right. Consider this a strategic phase of reinforcing your defences, ensuring that when you do decide to embrace more investment risk, you're leaping from a springboard of genuine strength and security, not from a place of vulnerability. This is you consciously and powerfully paving a smoother, more secure and infinitely more joyful path toward your unique *More Money, More Life* vision.

Your peace of mind is an invaluable asset

And then there's the crucial, often underestimated, factor of your emotional temperament. How would you react if you saw your investment values dip significantly in a short space of time? Would panic set in, prompting a sale at an inopportune moment? Or could you maintain your composure, anchored by your long-term vision and the emotional resilience you're cultivating? If the mere thought of market volatility ties your stomach in knots, a lower-risk strategy will serve your well-being far better, even if other factors might suggest a more adventurous path. Your peace of mind is an invaluable asset. Finally, your current knowledge and experience with investing play a part. If you're just stepping into this exciting world, it's perfectly sensible to begin with investments that carry lower to moderate risk, allowing you to learn and grow in confidence as you experience the market's rhythms.

To bring this home, ask yourself: if you had to rate your willingness to accept investment risk on a scale of one (extremely cautious) to ten (very adventurous, chasing high returns), where would you intuitively sit? If your total investments took a sudden 25% dive, what would be your gut reaction, your likely course of action? Honesty here is your greatest ally. Understanding your risk appetite isn't about sidestepping risk entirely; it's about engaging with it intelligently, choosing a path that allows you to sleep soundly at night while giving your money the fertile ground it needs to grow. It ensures your investment choices are a true reflection of you, preventing fear or greed from hijacking your carefully laid plans. And always remember, diversification – not putting all your eggs in one basket – is your steadfast friend in managing investment risk.

Exploring the tools of investment

For many people stepping into the world of investing, the sheer volume of options can feel overwhelming. The good news is you don't need to become a financial wizard overnight to start building wealth. Three of the most accessible and effective tools for beginner and experienced investors alike are index funds, Exchange Traded Funds (ETFs) and mutual funds. These vehicles are designed to make investing simpler and help you manage risk through diversification.

Think like a discerning, value-conscious shopper, not an impulsive gambler. Examine potential investments carefully, prioritize long-term utility and growth potential over short-term hype, diversify intelligently and only commit your capital when the value proposition feels undeniable and aligns with your risk tolerance.

For many people starting out, this might mean patiently researching and investing in low-cost index funds or Exchange Traded Funds (ETFs). These are investment products that hold a wide variety of stocks or bonds, essentially allowing you to buy a small piece of many different companies or assets with a single purchase.

Index funds: An index fund is a type of mutual fund or ETF that aims to replicate the performance of a specific market index, like the S&P 500 (which tracks 500 of the largest US companies) or the FTSE 100 (100 largest companies on the London Stock Exchange). Because they passively track an index rather than relying on a fund manager to pick winning stocks, they typically have very low management fees.

Think like a discerning, value-conscious shopper, not an impulsive gambler

ETFs (Exchange Traded Funds): ETFs are similar to index funds in that they often track an index and offer diversification. The main difference is how they're traded – ETFs trade on stock exchanges throughout the day like individual stocks, while traditional mutual funds are typically priced once at the end of the trading day.

Both index funds and ETFs offer instant diversification. Imagine trying to buy shares in all 500 companies in the S&P 500 individually; it would be complex and costly! With an S&P 500 index fund or ETF, you achieve that broad exposure in one go. This diversification is crucial because it spreads your risk; if one company in the fund performs poorly, its impact on your overall investment is cushioned by the performance of the other holdings. Their typically low management fees also mean more of your money stays invested and working for you. These features make them an excellent, simple way to participate in long-term market growth and are often recommended as a core holding for many investors.

Mutual funds: Think of a mutual fund as a collective investment. You, along with many other investors, pool your money together. This collective pot is then managed by a professional fund manager or a management team who make decisions about where and how to invest that money, according to the fund's specific objectives (e.g., growth, income, focus on a specific sector or geography).

The beauty of mutual funds lies in their inherent diversification (like ETFs, they typically invest in a wide range of assets, spreading your risk) and the option of professional management. If the thought of picking individual stocks or even specific ETFs feels daunting, a mutual fund can offer a more hands-off approach. Some are actively managed, meaning the fund manager and their team are actively researching, analysing and picking specific investments with the aim of outperforming a benchmark market index. Because of this active management and research, these funds often come with slightly higher fees (referred to as the expense ratio). Others are passively managed (like most index funds and many ETFs), aiming to simply replicate the performance of a particular market index. These typically have significantly lower fees due to the reduced overhead of active management.

For many people starting out, the simplicity and diversification offered by low-cost index funds, ETFs or well-chosen mutual funds make them an excellent gateway to building long-term wealth. They allow you to benefit from the growth of the broader market without needing to become an expert stock-picker yourself.

Investing in stocks and shares

You might also feel drawn to investing in individual companies. Perhaps you admire a company's innovative mission, you're a loyal customer of its products or you've done your research and see strong potential for its future growth. Investing in shares of individual companies means you become a part-owner of that business, however small your stake. If the company performs well and its profits grow, the value of your shares can increase (this is called capital appreciation). Additionally, many established companies share a portion of their profits with shareholders in the form of dividends, which can provide a regular income stream.

While picking individual stocks can feel more complex than buying a broad market fund, you don't need to be a Wall Street analyst to make informed choices. The key is to start with companies you understand and believe in, always applying the lens of understanding intrinsic worth (what the company is truly worth based on its fundamentals) and seeking a margin of safety (buying at a price that seems like a good value compared to its worth). As you delve into investing, you'll encounter various types of stocks. Understanding a couple of common distinctions can be helpful.

One key distinction is between cyclical and non-cyclical (or defensive) stocks. **Cyclical stocks** belong to companies whose fortunes tend to mirror economic cycles. Think of airlines, car manufacturers, luxury goods and construction. They often thrive when the economy is booming, offering the potential for high returns. However, this also means they carry higher volatility and risk, as their profits and stock prices can fall significantly during economic downturns. Conversely, **non-cyclical (or defensive) stocks** are associated with companies providing essential goods and services that people need regardless of the economic climate, such as utilities, food staples and healthcare. These tend to be more stable, often providing more consistent earnings and reliable dividends, though they may offer lower growth potential compared to cyclical stocks during economic upswings.

Another important comparison is between growth and value stocks. **Growth stocks** are shares in companies expected to expand at an above-average rate. These businesses, often in sectors like technology, typically reinvest their profits back into the company to fuel further expansion rather than paying out large dividends. While they offer high potential for significant capital appreciation if the company succeeds, they can also be more volatile and may trade at higher valuation multiples, their success heavily reliant on maintaining rapid growth. **Value stocks**, on the other hand, are shares in companies that appear to be trading for less than their intrinsic or fundamental worth. These might be established companies temporarily out of favour with the market or in industries not currently considered "hot". Value investors seek these perceived "bargains", anticipating good returns if the market eventually recognizes the company's true value. These stocks often pay higher dividends, but the risk is that the company might be undervalued for valid reasons (like a declining industry or poor management), and it could take a long time for its worth to be re-evaluated by the market, if ever.

Understanding these categories can help you align your individual stock choices with your risk tolerance and your overall financial goals. For instance, if you have a lower risk tolerance and are seeking more stable returns, you might lean toward non-cyclical and value stocks. If you have a higher risk tolerance and a longer time horizon, you might allocate a small portion of your portfolio to growth stocks.

Getting started and generating returns

You'll typically make these investments by buying stocks through an online brokerage account, similar to those used for the "easy investments" we discussed earlier. Many platforms offering ETFs and mutual funds also allow you to purchase shares in individual companies. The process is generally straightforward: open an account, fund it and then search for the stock you wish to buy using its unique ticker symbol (e.g., AAPL for Apple). Most platforms are designed to be very user-friendly.

Before diving into individual stocks, which inherently carry more risk than diversified funds, it's wise to ensure your financial foundation is solid. This means having an emergency fund covering three to six months of essential living expenses, a good handle on any high-interest debt like credit cards, and clear financial objectives, such as your BRIGHT goals (see pages 56–9). Crucially, only invest money in individual stocks that you can afford to potentially lose or tie-up for the long term, as the market can be volatile. Approach stock investing with a long-term mindset; it's generally not a path to quick riches. Remember, you don't need a fortune to begin; many brokers now offer fractional shares, allowing you to buy a small piece of a share and start learning with smaller amounts.

So, how do you actually make money from stocks? There are primarily two ways. The first is **capital appreciation**, which occurs when the price of the stock increases over time. If you buy a share for £100 and its value rises to £150, your investment has appreciated by £50 and selling it would then realize that profit (before any taxes or fees). This is often the main aim when investing in growth stocks.

The second way is through **dividends**. Many established, profitable companies choose to distribute a portion of their profits back to their shareholders. Think of these dividend payments, typically made quarterly or semi-annually, as your share of the company's success, paid directly into your brokerage account. Dividends can provide a regular income stream, or you can reinvest them to buy more shares, a powerful strategy for compounding your wealth over time. Companies that pay reliable, growing dividends are often favoured by investors seeking income and stability, and are frequently found among value and non-cyclical stocks. It's important to note that not all companies pay dividends; growth-focused companies, for instance, often reinvest all their profits back into the business to fuel further expansion.

The key to confident choices

Ultimately, as you choose these "easy investments" the key is to align them with your BRIGHT goals, your long-term vision and your deepest values. It's not just about picking a fund; it's about choosing investments that resonate with the abundant life you're building. For example, many platforms now simplify finding Environmental, Social and Governance (ESG) focused funds that reflect a commitment to positive impact.

Finally, always remember that patience is paramount in Precision Investing. It's far better to miss a fleeting, speculative opportunity than to risk your hard-earned capital on a dubious bet driven by hype or FOMO. Avoid chasing the hottest day-trading trends you see promoted on social media, especially those promising unrealistic rapid returns. True wealth building through investing is typically a marathon, not a sprint, and you're building something designed to last.

Pillar 3: The Citadel of Wealth

Financial strategies, no matter how brilliant, are ultimately useless without the mental and emotional fortitude to execute them consistently, especially under pressure. Your mind is the command centre of your Citadel of Wealth. This pillar is about forging an unbreakable inner stronghold, one that's impervious to the inevitable storms of market volatility, fear-driven impulses and the seductive siren song of doubt or greed.

Mastery here begins with cultivating emotional detachment. Not a cold indifference, but a clear-eyed, calm awareness that you can nurture through practices like mindfulness and meditation. Learn to observe your fear when markets dip, or your excitement when they surge, without immediately obeying those emotions. Start simply; notice your emotional reaction to financial news or market swings without judgement. Acknowledge the feeling, then bring your focus back to your long-term strategy and core values. Ensure every significant financial decision aligns with these deepest values; this alignment is the ultimate source of true resilience and peace of mind.

But don't attempt to build this fortress alone. Seek your tribe; trusted mentors who have wisdom and experience, supportive masterminds with whom you can share challenges and strategies, and like-minded peers who both challenge your thinking and champion your growth. This carefully curated network reinforces your resolve, sharpens your strategy and provides invaluable perspective during uncertain times. And finally, commit to continuous evolution. Feed your mind with sound financial knowledge, consistently refine your approaches based on experience and evidence (not emotion), and always lead your financial life with unwavering integrity. Wealth built upon this unshakeable foundation isn't just about accumulating numbers, it becomes a lasting legacy that reflects your enduring principles and inner strength.

> Financial strategies, no matter how brilliant, are ultimately useless without the mental and emotional fortitude to execute them consistently

These pillars aren't isolated strategies; they're dynamically interconnected gears in your Evergreen Wealth Engine. **Digital Mastery** can generate the robust cash flow needed to fuel your **Precision Investing**. Your **Citadel of Wealth** provides the essential emotional resilience required to execute both your digital and investment strategies with clarity, discipline and unwavering long-term commitment. Together, they create a powerful, self-reinforcing cycle of sustainable growth and ever-expanding abundance.

Weathering life's financial storms

The journey to a *More Money, More Life* existence is an exhilarating adventure, filled with growth, creation and empowerment. But no adventure is without its unexpected tempests. You've learned to master your mindset, build your Evergreen Wealth Engine and execute with precision. Yet, life can, and often will, throw curveballs that test even the strongest foundations. A sudden job loss, a nerve-wracking market crash or an unforeseen expense that lands like a lightning bolt.

You've heard my own story of being scammed by a builder, a crisis that forced me to confront my deepest financial fears and ultimately rebuild from the ground up. That experience taught me that resilience isn't just about enduring; it's about transforming adversity into a catalyst for even greater strength. While your specific challenges may differ, the core principles of navigating financial setbacks and emerging stronger are universal. This is about equipping your "Citadel of Wealth" not just with strong walls, but with shock absorbers and a well-practised recovery drill.

Your first responder in a crisis

Before we dive into specific scenarios, know that the origin of all financial recovery is your mindset. When a storm hits, you first acknowledge the reality of the setback with courage and clarity, without sinking into blame or shame over what you "should have" done. Then, in the midst of what can feel like chaos, you seize your controllables. It's easy to feel powerless, but by laser-focusing your energy on what you can control – your actions, your responses, your next small step – you reclaim your power. Every setback, however painful, also carries a potent lesson; approach it with curiosity, asking "What can I learn from this? How can this experience make me wiser, more strategic, more resilient?" This transforms challenges into teachers. And throughout it all, practise radical self-compassion. Recovering from a financial blow takes time and energy, so treat yourself with the same kindness you'd offer a dear friend. This isn't a weakness; it's essential fuel for your comeback.

Navigating the storms

Armed with this resilient mindset, let's explore how to navigate some common financial challenges.

If you face the unsettling impact of job loss, it may feel like the ground has vanished. Your first move is swift financial triage. Take a deep breath, calmly assess your immediate cash flow and dust off that Zero-Based Budget we discussed (see page 61), identifying essential expenses versus those you can temporarily pause. This is precisely why we built that all-important emergency fund. It's your financial hurricane shelter, designed to give you breathing room. Immediately activate your network, polish that personal brand (see Chapter 6) and explore all avenues for new income, whether it's your next dream role or temporary "scrappy capital" streams to bridge the gap. Your skills and inherent resourcefulness are your greatest assets here.

> Every setback, however painful, also carries a potent lesson

Then there's the anxiety of riding out investment market storms. Watching your hard-earned investments plummet during a downturn can churn your stomach, and the primal urge might be to panic and sell. This is where your "Citadel of Wealth" and the emotional detachment we've cultivated become your superpower. Resist that urge to react impulsively. Anchor yourself by remembering your long-term BRIGHT goals (see pages 56–9) and the risk tolerance you consciously aligned with (see page 114). For most long-term investors, "staying the course", rather than attempting to time the market's wild swings, has historically proven to be a sound strategy. While unsettling, market downturns can present opportunities, allowing you to acquire quality assets at lower prices. But the primary objective during any storm is to shield your long-term vision from the grip of short-term fear.

What about when life throws an unexpected financial haymaker, like a sudden medical emergency, an urgent home repair or a family crisis demanding significant funds? These can rock even the best-laid plans. Again, your emergency fund is your first courageous line of defence, designed to absorb such shocks. If it doesn't quite cover it, take a calm moment to assess all your options before rushing into high-interest debt. Could you temporarily reallocate funds from other goals? Are there assets you could leverage, or support available from your network or community? Once the immediate crisis is managed, revisit your budget and savings plan with renewed focus, determined to rebuild that vital financial buffer.

Your comeback

No matter the nature of the setback, the path to recovery involves a clear blueprint for action. Start with a full and frank assessment to get a crystal-clear picture of the financial impact, because knowledge, even when tough, is power. Then, craft your recovery plan. Just like your BRIGHT goals, your comeback needs clear, measurable and achievable steps to get you back on your feet. Break it down into manageable actions. And crucially, lean on your "constellation". You are not alone. This is the time to reach out to trusted mentors, financial advisors or your supportive community (as we'll explore with such excitement in Chapter 10). Sharing the burden can lighten the load and often brings invaluable fresh perspectives and solutions. Finally, acknowledge every single step forward. Recovery is a journey, not a sprint, so celebrate the small wins along the way. Each positive step rebuilds not just your finances, but your confidence and unstoppable momentum.

Financial setbacks are not a sign of failure; they're an inevitable part of a life lived fully and a wealth journey pursued with ambition. They're the tests that forge your resilience, deepen your wisdom and, ultimately, prove the unshakeable strength of your *More Money, More Life* foundation. Each storm weathered doesn't just mean you've survived, it means you've learned, adapted, and are now even more powerfully equipped to command your destiny.

Your wealth journey, no matter your starting point

So, you're fired up about the Evergreen Wealth Engine! You can see the vision. Assets working for you, income streams flowing and a life designed with true financial freedom. But perhaps a voice inside whispers, "This sounds incredible, Sarah, but I'm drowning in debt right now" or "My income barely covers my bills, how could I possibly build an 'engine'?" Your starting point does not define your destiny. That feeling of being overwhelmed when financial foundations are shaky is real, and I honour it. Many of us, myself included, have navigated those treacherous waters. But the Evergreen Wealth Engine isn't a concept reserved for the already wealthy; it's a pathway available to anyone with the courage to claim it, the grit to build it and the wisdom to start, even if that start feels incredibly small.

Before we even talk about pounds and pence, the very first "capital" you need to cultivate is a steadfast belief that this is possible for you. We've talked extensively about rewriting your money story, and nowhere is this more critical than when you're facing what feels like a mountain. That scarcity mindset, the one that tells you "There's never enough" or "I'll always be

> Your journey to an Evergreen Wealth Engine begins not in your bank account, but in the fertile ground of your mind

stuck", is the heaviest anchor. You must consciously, fiercely cut it loose. Your journey to an Evergreen Wealth Engine begins not in your bank account, but in the fertile ground of your mind. Declare that you're capable, resourceful and destined for more. This firm belief is the foundation upon which all tangible progress will be built.

If significant high-interest debt is part of your current reality, see it for what it is – a direct drain on your future engine's fuel. Every pound paid in interest to someone else is a pound not working for you. Remember our discussions in Chapter 3 on "Abundance Unlocked" and the power of intentional budgeting? Those principles are your weapons here. Whether you chose the Snowball Method for those quick motivational wins or the Avalanche Method to save the most on interest, attacking that debt with relentless focus isn't just about getting out of a hole; it's about actively reclaiming capital. Every reduced debt payment frees up future cash flow. Think of this as uncovering the first trickles of oil for your engine.

Your launchpad fund

Now, let's talk about creating that initial seed money, even when things feel tight. This is where "scrappy" meets strategy. Your first line of attack is to create micro-surpluses with mighty impact. Revisit your Zero-Based Budget (see page 61) with a new, laser-focused mission, to intentionally carve out a small, consistent "Engine Launchpad Fund". Even £10, £20 or £50 a month, when consciously allocated and fiercely protected, begins to build incredible momentum. It's not about the initial sum; it's about cultivating the potent habit of prioritizing your engine.

Next, unleash your existing skills. Your very first income lever. Before you even think about building a full-scale "Digital Mastery" asset, what unique talents do you already possess that could generate a swift income boost? Are you a whiz at writing, a genius at organizing, a maestro in the kitchen, a gifted teacher or brilliant at fixing things? Consider offering freelance services, taking on a few gig-work projects in your spare hours or providing micro-consulting. This isn't necessarily about launching your forever business right now; it's about strategically leveraging what you have today to generate cash. This cash can then be immediately channelled into your Engine Launchpad Fund or used to obliterate debt even faster. Think of this as an early, empowering taste of "Your Magnet for More Money" (Chapter 6), claiming and valuing your innate skills from day one.

If you're contemplating a side hustle, make it the strategic side hustle launchpad. Choose it with your Evergreen Wealth Engine clearly in mind. Can you ignite something with minimal upfront cost that either directly generates cash for your Engine Launchpad Fund or, just as importantly, helps you build skills and assets crucial for one of the main engine pillars later on? Perhaps this initial side hustle's primary purpose is purely to create that first £500 or £1,000 launchpad. Its mission is to fuel the bigger, bolder vision. And sometimes, a short, intense period of the focused frugality sprint can be an incredibly powerful way to accumulate that small launch fund with speed and precision. This isn't about adopting a lifelong deprivation mindset, which only stifles your abundant energy. Instead, frame it as a dedicated, time-bound sprint with a clear financial target. Perhaps saving an extra £X in the next three to six months. Knowing it's temporary and serves a magnificent purpose can transform it into an exhilarating challenge rather than a punishment.

Bridging scarcity to systemic growth

Imagine Maria, a talented writer buried under student loan debt and working a demanding but low-paying job. Her Evergreen dream felt distant, almost impossible. But she decided to start fiercely. She adopted the Snowball Method for her debt, carving out an extra £75 a month. Simultaneously, she used her exceptional writing skills to take on two small freelance blog-writing gigs each month, earning an additional £150. Every single penny of that £225 went into her "Engine Launchpad Fund". After a year of this dedicated effort, she had cleared her most expensive debt and accumulated over £1,000. This wasn't millions, but it was her hard-won capital, a testament to her resolve. With it, she invested in a high-quality course to learn how to create and market her own writing workshops (hello, Pillar 1: Digital Mastery!) and made her very first £100 investment into a low-cost index fund (igniting Pillar 2: Precision Investing). The engine hadn't just sputtered; it had roared into life.

This is how your journey begins. That "launchpad capital", whether it's £100 or £1,000, becomes the precious resource you then strategically deploy. It might be the money to invest in a crucial skill or course that empowers you to build your first digital product, or to cover the minimal software and tools needed for your burgeoning online venture. Perhaps it's the fund that allows you to make those initial, small but powerful investments into a diversified fund. Or it could even be the key to freeing up enough of your precious time, perhaps by allowing you to reduce hours at a soul-crushing job if that income is replaced by a more aligned side-hustle, so you can focus your energy on building your engine's core components.

Ignite your wealth engine

The journey from a tight financial spot to building a thriving Evergreen Wealth Engine is undoubtedly a testament to your resolve. It requires discipline, creativity and a commitment to your vision. But it is absolutely, unequivocally possible. The strategies we've discussed are not about wishful thinking; they are practical, actionable steps designed to help you build that crucial initial momentum. Every small surplus saved, every extra pound earned and allocated to your Engine Fund, every debt payment conquered, is a victory.

It's a declaration that you're the architect of your financial future. The Evergreen Wealth Engine is not a distant dream; it's a powerful reality you begin to construct today, with the resources you have, right where you are.

Take that first brave, scrappy step. Your engine, and the *More Money, More Life* future it promises, is waiting for you to turn the key. So, now you're ready to unleash this incredible potential, let's get into breaking free from the old paradigms, escape the grind and begin constructing your solid foundation of true wealth. Your Ikonic life isn't gifted; it's meticulously, joyfully built. And now that we've laid the groundwork, plumbed the depths of your money mindset and ignited your financial vision, the true alchemy begins. It's time to bridge the exhilarating gap between dreaming and doing. You now hold the powerful blueprint for your Evergreen Wealth Engine. But even the most sophisticated engine remains dormant without fuel, and the most brilliant vision remains unseen without a powerful signal to the world. The next chapter, "Your Magnet for More Money", is your guide to becoming the magnetic force that attracts the opportunities, clients and capital needed to ignite it all. Prepare to become undeniable.

CHAPTER 6

YOUR MAGNET FOR MORE MONEY

In the last chapter, we architected your Evergreen Wealth Engine, a powerful system designed to generate enduring wealth and unlock true financial independence. We've laid down the blueprint for assets that work for you, building a foundation for stability and growth. But even the most sophisticated engine remains idle without fuel. The most brilliant portfolio is impotent if opportunity remains unaware of its existence. What good is a meticulously crafted engine if the keys to ignite it – the deals, the capital, the synergistic partnerships – remain elusive?

Knowing the "how" of wealth generation is critical, but insight without activation is worthless. Leaving opportunity to chance is a gamble, a coin toss against circumstance. So, we arrive at the crucial question, the one that separates the architects of destiny from the bystanders waiting for luck. How do we eliminate chance from the equation? How do we engineer a presence so magnetic, so undeniable, that success becomes a foregone conclusion? This requires a profound shift in your thinking and your execution. We move beyond the tangible assets discussed in the Evergreen Wealth Engine and delve into the potent, often underestimated power of who you are in the marketplace. This is where we construct Your Magnet for More Money.

This requires a profound shift in your thinking and your execution. We move beyond the tangible assets discussed in the Evergreen Wealth Engine and delve into the potent, often underestimated power of who you are in the marketplace. This is where we construct Your Magnet for More Money.

Let's obliterate the superficial aspect of "personal branding" right now. This journey isn't about crafting some polished, palatable online persona designed for public consumption or chasing the fleeting dopamine hit of vanity metrics like likes and follows. We are not here to be merely popular; we are here to become undeniably powerful. We are here to step into our roles as the sought-after, unmistakable authorities in our fields, the go-to experts whose names become synonymous with tangible results and profound transformation. This chapter is about consciously engineering influence, leveraging your authentic personal brand not just to be seen, but to attract premium-priced clients if you're an entrepreneur, or command the higher salary and opportunities you deserve if you're rocking the corporate world. Consider why a globally recognized expert can command fees many times higher than a less-known practitioner offering seemingly similar services. It's the potent force of their established brand, meticulously built on proven results, insightful thought leadership and hard-earned trust. Trust that signals undeniable value and magnetizes premium opportunities. That's the power of the brand we're building here. It's about meticulously constructing a presence so magnetic, so authentically potent, that the right opportunities don't just knock, they kick down your door, demanding an audience with you.

It's about meticulously constructing a presence so magnetic, so authentically potent, that the right opportunities don't just knock, they kick down your door

Forget passively "building a following". That paradigm is dying. We're creating an irresistible gravitational pull in today's overwhelmingly noisy economy, where attention is the new currency. A pull that only you, with your distinct genius and unique value proposition, can generate.

The old story, the one that keeps countless brilliant minds shackled to the grind, screams, "Trade your precious time for money! Hustle harder! Sacrifice more! Prove your worth through sheer, exhausting effort!" This is the narrative of the 9-to-5 (or often, the 9-to-9) where your income is capped by the hours you can physically work, where your potential is dictated by a job description, and where your financial security rests precariously on the decisions of others. It's a system that often values presence over performance, and conformity over creativity, leading to a slow drain of your most vibrant energy. That game is fundamentally rigged. It's designed to keep you perpetually running, chasing a horizon that forever recedes. We're not playing that game. Our truth, the one that unlocks exponential wealth, leads to authentic freedom.

Your personal brand IS your ultimate wealth-generating asset

Imagine your personal brand as a self-replicating engine of influence, compounding value while you sleep, finally severing the archaic chains of the billable hour. This isn't about slick marketing slogans or fleeting productivity hacks. It's about embodying a promise, projecting a value so compelling, so intrinsically you, that opportunity relentlessly hunts you down. It seeks your specific genius, your unique solutions, your leadership. It's about architecting a future where your influence, your impact and your financial trajectory are no longer subject to luck or circumstance, but become the inevitable consequence of the powerful, intentional brand you've meticulously built.

Your personal brand is not simply narrative – it is currency. In the new world, visibility wields power; presence becomes possibility. Each post, each connection, each idea offered in truth is a quiet investment – an unseen seed – growing, compounding, blossoming into legacy. This is not vanity; it is vision, the courage to stand in the light, to build meaning in the open, to turn reputation into a reservoir of trust. When you nurture your brand, you draw the world nearer; aligned opportunities find their way to you, and new paths to wealth and impact appear. The *More Money, More Life* philosophy sees your brand as the foundation of abundance, not built on performance, but on the steady heartbeat of purpose. For when your voice is true, it does more than open doors for you; it opens them for all those you are meant to serve.

Confront the stark reality – without a commanding, authentic brand your wealth potential is perpetually throttled. You're attempting to accelerate with the emergency brake firmly on, suffocating the vital oxygen of trust and visibility required for any significant growth. In today's deafening digital landscape, trust isn't merely important; it's the ultimate, scarcest currency. Your brand, when built with integrity and clarity, becomes the finely-tuned signal that cuts through the pervasive static. It earns that invaluable trust, forges genuine human connection and, ultimately, unlocks the doors to the deals, partnerships and opportunities that build empires. It becomes the magnetic force field drawing in your ideal clients, your fiercest advocates and the strategic collaborators who will amplify your mission.

Understand this deeply; wealth amassed without a resonant legacy leaves a hollow echo. It's a towering skyscraper erected on shifting sand. Your brand provides the granite foundation upon which lasting impact is constructed. It's the story that reverberates long after the financial transactions fade, a living testament to the value you created, the lives you irrevocably transformed, the positive

Your brand provides the granite foundation upon which lasting impact is constructed change you sparked in the world. So, refuse to play their game any longer. Stop hustling for scraps according to patriarchal rules designed to keep you small. Building your Ikonic brand is your ultimate act of strategic defiance. It's the mechanism by which you rewrite the rules, definitively own your category and become utterly irreplaceable. It requires defining your unique genius with piercing clarity, articulating your undeniable value proposition, and wielding it all with such conviction that the market simply will recognize your brilliance and reward you accordingly.

Knowing this intellectually, understanding the strategic imperative, is different from embodying it after facing the raw, often brutal realities of putting yourself out there. Allow me to pull back the curtain on a time when this magnetic presence wasn't my reality, but a hard-won insight forged in the crucible of entrepreneurial struggle. When I first made the leap from the gilded cage of the corporate world, the feeling was sheer, untamed liberation. Freedom! I had all the strategies, the skills sharpened over years, the boundless, kinetic energy of a newly uncaged spirit. What I lacked, with painful, glaring lucidity, were the clients. Those initial months became a visceral, humbling masterclass in the vast difference between possessing expertise and being recognized for that expertise.

I vividly recall pouring my soul into masterclasses, dedicating nights and weekends to client work. The feedback was consistently exceptional. "Game-changing", clients would effuse, their eyes alight with newfound clarity. The value exchange was undeniably potent. Yet, the client pipeline felt like a cruel lottery, a stomach-lurching gamble. Cash flow wasn't flowing at all; it was a terrifying rollercoaster plunging through darkness. Dizzying peaks one month, gut-wrenching drops the next, leaving me breathless with anxiety, crying on the kitchen floor in a crumpled heap. You simply cannot build an empire from that precarious ledge, constantly scanning the horizon in desperation, forcing smiles through gritted teeth at endless networking events, ticking off all the supposed "right" things while feeling like you're sprinting backward on a treadmill. This was compounded by a rapidly evolving market. With AI democratizing content creation and a surge in online "gurus", the personal development and coaching space became flooded. Promises of get-rich-quick schemes, courses touted as solving all the world's problems, and coaching packages that guaranteed millionaire status for a five-minute strategy were everywhere. You get the picture. The market, rightly so, had become incredibly sceptical. Potential clients were wary, making it extraordinarily challenging for new entrants, or even established players without a trusted brand, to cut through the noise, let alone command premium fees and reach milestones like the magical £100,000 mark.

The real chokehold on my progress wasn't a lack of skill, confidence or even a relentless, bordering-on-unhealthy work ethic. It was something far more insidious. Invisibility in a deafening sea of noise. I was the best-kept secret in my own burgeoning field. I vividly recall a well-intentioned coach urging, "Just push through, Sarah, do it for your children!" as if sheer desperation was the strategy I'd somehow missed. It wasn't. The truth was, the ground beneath us had shifted. Potential clients were becoming savvier, more discerning and rightly sceptical after waves of empty online promises from others. The path to earning trust, especially for high-value, transformative work, had become a steeper, longer climb.

The journey of establishing genuine credibility and demonstrating undeniable authority demanded far more than mere competence. It demanded being seen, being heard and, crucially, being trusted. And believe me, it's no different in the corporate world. Without a strong internal brand, without being known for your unique value, your unwavering reliability, your innovative spark, you can be the most talented individual in your department, yet find yourself consistently overlooked. That promotion, that pay rise, that career-defining project? They'll pass you by. You remain a hidden gem, your brilliance maddeningly unseen by those holding the keys to your advancement.

Perhaps this resonates with your own journey. Regardless of your industry, you're likely navigating a similar sea of overwhelming sameness. Hundreds, maybe thousands, offer services or products that appear superficially similar. In this crowded arena, standing out isn't merely advantageous, it's fundamental to survival. It demands cultivating a laser focus, becoming utterly synonymous with the unique transformation you deliver and broadcasting your signal – your core message, your value – with such piercing clarity and consistency that it slices through the noise. So, how do you escape the exhausting scramble? You stop chasing. You start attracting. You consciously, strategically, relentlessly engineer an **Ikonic Personal Brand**.

For me, the epiphany wasn't instantaneous but a gradual, persistent dawning. I began to recognize I'd unconsciously laid fragments of the foundation for years, stepping onto industry stages to share hard-won insights, building trust frameworks in the boardroom and genuine relationships without an immediate "ask", consistently offering value simply out of passion for my craft. The quantum leap occurred when I consciously chose to systematize this, to amplify it intentionally, and crucially, to start openly teaching the very process of building authority that I was painstakingly mastering myself. That decision became the fulcrum upon which everything shifted. My online presence went bonkers, particularly on professional platforms like LinkedIn. Leads began flowing to me, appearing like magic in my inbox from prospects I hadn't pursued. The frantic, soul-crushing grind for business began to dissolve. I consciously tuned out the cacophony of conflicting "expert" advice and focused intently on the clear signals the market was sending. Build your platform, amplify your authentic voice, own your authority.

This path wasn't without its detours. My company Dream Catcher was my third baby, a venture I initially built as a side hustle, fuelled by the "seed capital" from my day job. When I left corporate, it was ignited with that intoxicating post-freedom buzz. But as those initial funds dwindled and the stark reality of being the family breadwinner set in, I succumbed to the entrepreneur's primal fear. I started chasing the money. Scarcity became my strategist. I jumped at fleeting trends, compromised my core offerings, said "yes" to misaligned projects, all driven by a tightening knot of fear. The more desperate I felt, the harder I pushed, and ironically, the less magnetic I became. It was a painful vortex, fuelled not by lack of motivation, but by operating from a place of deep-seated fear and lack. The ultimate repellent to abundance.

The pivot, the true moment I regained escape velocity, was when I consciously shifted my entire operational focus from desperately selling to authentically serving from the core of my brand and the value I stood for, the brand I was now intentionally cultivating. That's when the internal landscape shifted, the crippling financial anxiety began to loosen its grip and I started designing offers and products that felt profoundly aligned, authentically powerful and, consequently, attracted the right clients and the right opportunities with astonishing ease.

> It's about being so good, so clear and so visible in your niche that opportunities naturally gravitate toward your undeniable expertise and authority

So, let's get ruthlessly tactical. Because this isn't just about lofty concepts; it's about engineering your bespoke system for attracting opportunity. It's about forging your blazing force, the mechanism that bends the market toward you, liberating you permanently from the soul-crushing anxiety of an unpredictable future. We operate in an attention economy; visibility alone is noise. We're constructing a reality where your influence is undeniable, pervasive. We're architects of inevitability. This is how those public-speaking engagements begin to flow, how joint venture partnerships land in your inbox, how media outlets seek your opinion. It happens because you've built a reputation, a body of work, a clear message that resonates so powerfully that people want to be associated with your brand. The "how" involves consistently delivering exceptional value through your platforms, engaging authentically with your audience, strategically networking with key collaborators, and positioning your insights in a way that establishes you as a thought leader. It's about being so good, so clear, and so visible in your niche that opportunities naturally gravitate toward your undeniable expertise and authority.

Forget the old paradigm of trading time for money. Your personal brand is your appreciating asset, the engine compounding value while you dedicate your energy to delivering your highest impact. We're not merely building résumés here; we're consciously crafting legends. This is the playbook. The system honed through my own trials, errors and relentless refinement. This is IKONIC™, the ultimate framework for engineering industry authority.

The six pillars of IKONIC™ leadership

The IKONIC™ framework

You are brilliant at what you do. The problem? You are still the industry's best-kept secret.

We believe true influence isn't about shouting louder; it's about engineering the authority that makes you the only one worth listening to. It's the strategic shift from chasing opportunities to being the one who is pursued.

The IKONIC™ Framework is our proprietary "ology", the systematic approach to becoming unignorable, irreplaceable and the sought-after choice in your industry. It's not about being known everywhere; it's about being undeniable where it matters.

I – Impact-driven identity

This is where you stop competing and start defining the narrative. We eradicate generic labels and carve out your unique category of one, transforming you from "an advisor" into "the definitive authority" in your niche. Your identity becomes so clear and your impact so profound that it makes competition irrelevant. This is the foundational work that allows you to attract your ideal high-net-worth (HNW) clients effortlessly.

K – Knowledge-driven credibility engine

This is the engine that builds trust while you sleep. We build your fortress of credibility brick by brick, using strategic podcast appearances, a dominant LinkedIn presence and powerful thought leadership that shapes industry conversation. We engineer your authority so profoundly that choosing you becomes the only logical, intelligent decision for high-calibre clients.

O – Opportunity architecture

Forget random networking. This is about engineering strategic collisions that bring high-value opportunities to your door. By intentionally constructing a powerful ecosystem of collaborators, referral partners and media platforms, we position you at the centre of your industry's most important conversations. Your network becomes an automated asset

> Visibility isn't achieved by shouting louder; it's about showing up powerfully, authentically and consistently

that exponentially amplifies your reach and accelerates your trajectory.

N – Narrative power

Your story is the currency of human connection. We weave your origin, your expertise and your bold vision for the future into a compelling narrative that connects on a human level. This story transforms you from another expert into the only guide your ideal client trusts to lead them. Visibility isn't achieved by shouting louder; it's about showing up powerfully, authentically and consistently, It's the magnetic force that pulls ideal clients in, turning passive observers into fervent believers.

I – Influence at scale

This is how you become unignorable to the right people. We take your powerful narrative and ensure it achieves strategic omnipresence, meeting your ideal audience where they already congregate. By repurposing your core message across the right channels with lethal effectiveness, your influence compounds. You stop shouting into the void and start being the sought-after voice your market is actively seeking.

C – Consistency that converts

This is the key to a lasting legacy. True authority isn't forged in a weekend; it's the earned result of relentless consistency in your message, your values and your presence. We build sustainable systems and workflows that allow you to maintain your presence with ease. This dependability creates profound trust, builds unstoppable momentum, and ensures your brand works for you for decades to come, giving you the freedom to enjoy the life it creates. Cement your influence so profoundly that choosing you becomes the only logical, intelligent decision.

I	**Impact-driven identity** Design who you are, not just what you do. Craft a powerful personal presence that reflects your truth and commands attention.
K	**Knowledge-driven credibility engine** Build a reputation so trusted it opens doors before you arrive.
O	**Opportunity architecture** Become the signal, not the noise. Attract high-value rooms, roles and relationships that elevate your future.
N	**Narrative power** Craft your real story as your ultimate differentiator, your strongest strategic asset: instinctive, human, and unforgettable.
I	**Influence at scale** Don't just speak, shift thinking. Use your voice to set the tone, move markets and lead conversations that matter.
C	**Consistency that converts** Lead with rhythm. Show up boldly, again and again, until you're not just known, you're expected.

The IKONIC personal brand framework

This is the long game. The "how" here involves creating sustainable systems for your content creation and engagement. Batch-create content, develop a content calendar, repurpose core ideas across different platforms, and build a small, reliable team or leverage tools if needed as you grow. It's about building habits and processes that ensure you can maintain your authentic presence and value delivery over years, not just weeks or months. How will you sustain this momentum and remain powerfully relevant for decades to come?

The IKONIC™ Blueprint

You are already an expert. This blueprint is the first step in the strategic process of transforming your expertise from the industry's "best-kept secret" into undeniable authority. Use these prompts to begin the work of defining your narrative and commanding your legacy.

I – Impact-driven identity

This is where you stop competing and start defining your category of one.

- My category of one (I am not just a/an ... I am THE ...)
- The specific transformation I engineer
- My ideal HNW audience (Who must I be undeniable to?)
- The legacy I will create (The dent I am here to make)

K – Knowledge-driven credibility engine

This is how you build the proof that makes you the only logical choice.

- Core insights that Prove my authority
- My authority platforms (Where my voice will shape the conversation)
- My fortress of trust (The social proof – case studies, testimonials – I will cultivate)

O – Opportunity architecture

This is where you stop chasing and start attracting.

- My high-value ecosystem (The key people, podcasts and platforms that matter)
- My strategy for engineering strategic collisions (How I will connect with value)

N – Narrative power

This is the story that connects, builds trust and positions you as the guide.

- My origin story (The relevant "why" behind my expertise)
- My core philosophy (The disruptive belief that guides my work)
- The compelling story only I can tell

I – Influence at scale

This is how you become unignorable to the people who can hire, fund, or champion you.

- Primary channels (Where my ideal HNW audience congregates)
- My plan for consistent, high-value content that cuts through the noise

C – Consistency that onverts

This is how you build a legacy, not just a moment.

- My core message (The single idea I will own and repeat)
- My systems for a sustainable presence (The habits that will ensure longevity)
- How I will remain the undeniable choice for decades to come

This IKONIC™ system is your strategic differentiator. It's the dividing line between those caught in the endless hamster wheel of hustle and those who command their category, dominate their niche and become the irreplaceable architects of their own abundant destiny. It's the mechanism for transforming you from A choice into THE choice. It's, fundamentally, how you build your magnet.

Forging your Ikonic brand is not just a strategy; it's your sacred initiation into engineering the authentic wealth, profound impact, and exhilarating freedom you were truly meant for. This is the unshakeable bedrock upon which your lasting success and meaningful legacy are not just built, but beautifully and boldly sculpted.

My client, Hannah, was the classic "industry's best-kept secret". An accomplished real estate broker with immense talent, she was watching less qualified competitors own the narrative that should have been hers.

The moment she committed to the IKONIC™ Framework, we began the work of engineering her authority.

- **Impact-Driven Identity:** First, we defined her unique category of one. She was no longer just "a real estate broker"; she became "the trusted advisor for securing off-market legacy properties for HNW families". She staked her claim on a specific, high-value territory where trust is non-negotiable.
- **Knowledge-Driven Credibility Engine:** Next, we built her fortress of trust. She shared potent market intelligence and undeniable social proof through discreet case studies of client success, making her the only logical choice for discerning clients.
- **Opportunity Architecture:** We engineered strategic collisions, placing her trusted voice on high-impact podcasts focused on wealth management and luxury lifestyles, where her ideal clients were already listening. The right opportunities stopped being random; they became inevitable.

- **Narrative Power:** She crafted a compelling narrative around her core philosophy: that property is not just a transaction, but a pillar of a family's legacy. This wasn't just content; it was the currency of human connection that built a deep, authentic bond with her audience.
- **Influence at Scale:** Her narrative was then amplified with Intentional Omnipresence. Consistent, high-value LinkedIn posts showcasing her unique perspective cut through the noise, resonated deeply, and sparked conversations with family offices and wealth advisors.
- **Consistency that Converts:** Finally, her weekly newsletter, offering insights into legacy properties, became a non-negotiable read for her target audience. This relentless consistency built compounding momentum and cemented her status as a true authority.

The result is that Hannah is no longer the best-kept secret. She is the sought-after authority in her field. She stopped competing and started defining the narrative, attracting a continuous pipeline of dream HNW clients ready to invest in her vision and expertise.

Similarly, in the corporate world, think of my old team member, let's call him Bob. He was a high-integrity executive with a powerful vision, but he was the classic "best-kept secret" within his own firm, watching less strategic thinkers get the promotions he deserved.

When he began applying the IKONIC™ Framework to his career, the trajectory shifted.

- **Impact-Driven Identity:** He first defined his unique category of one. He was no longer a mid-level manager; he was the internal leader driving innovative sustainability practices to create tangible efficiencies and boost team morale.
- **Knowledge-Driven Credibility Engine:** He built his fortress of trust by leading successful pilot projects and meticulously documenting their outcomes. When he presented his findings

to leadership, he wasn't just sharing data; he was shaping the conversation around the future of the business.

- **Opportunity Architecture:** He engineered strategic collisions with senior leadership, seeking mentorship and seizing challenging cross-functional initiatives that increased his visibility and proved his capabilities beyond his role.
- **Narrative Power:** He meticulously crafted his internal narrative, becoming known as the company's passionate "sustainability champion". His story positioned him as the trusted guide for this critical business evolution.
- **Influence at Scale:** Through compelling presentations and company-wide communications, he achieved Intentional Omnipresence. He ensured the right decision-makers consistently saw his vision and the value he delivered.
- **Consistency that Converts:** His steadfast dedication and follow-through were undeniable. This relentless consistency built compounding momentum for his internal brand.

The result was that Bob was no longer just doing his job; he was defining the narrative of his own career. His promotion wasn't just a possibility; it became the inevitable consequence of an Ikonic internal brand that made him the undeniable choice for leadership.

The real question isn't if you possess the capability – you absolutely do – it's when will you choose to step fully into your power and begin architecting your inevitable success? But the blueprint alone isn't enough. The path forward demands translating this architecture into tangible, consistent action. It requires amplifying your reach strategically and ensuring your influence not only lands but endures. It demands commitment, disciplined execution and the profound courage to fully step into the powerful, Ikonic presence you're destined to embody.

Having laid this foundation, having claimed your Ikonic potential, the next vital stage is mastering the art of bringing it all to life. Prepare to move beyond the blueprint and into masterful action, because the next chapter unveils the Art of Execution.

CHAPTER 7
THE ART OF EXECUTION

Many dream, but few execute. It's the yawning chasm between aspiration and achievement that truly separates the casual visionaries from the relentless doers, the architects of their own destiny. Forget the vague corporate jargon and tired, dusty clichés. In this chapter, we're not just setting goals; we're engineering success. This is about taking your wildest, most audacious ambitions and forging them into your lived reality, using my powerhouse **MORE Framework: Motivation, Obstacles, Resources, Execution.** We're systematically turning your aspirations into non-negotiable realities. There's no room for hesitation here, just pure, focused, relentless momentum as we craft the unshakeable architecture for your financial and personal triumph. This isn't just about getting things done; it's about achieving what truly matters, with precision and passion.

Motivation: dreams to reality

Motivation isn't just some fleeting spark, a momentary burst of enthusiasm that fades with the first headwind. True motivation, the kind that propels empires and fuels legacies, is a sustainable, dynamic and deeply internal force. It's the heartbeat of your ambition. In earlier chapters, you've courageously explored the profound "why" behind your BRIGHT goals. Now, it's time to learn how to sustain that sacred fire, to keep your engine roaring with unstoppable power through every inevitable twist, turn and seeming detour on your journey. This section is about igniting your

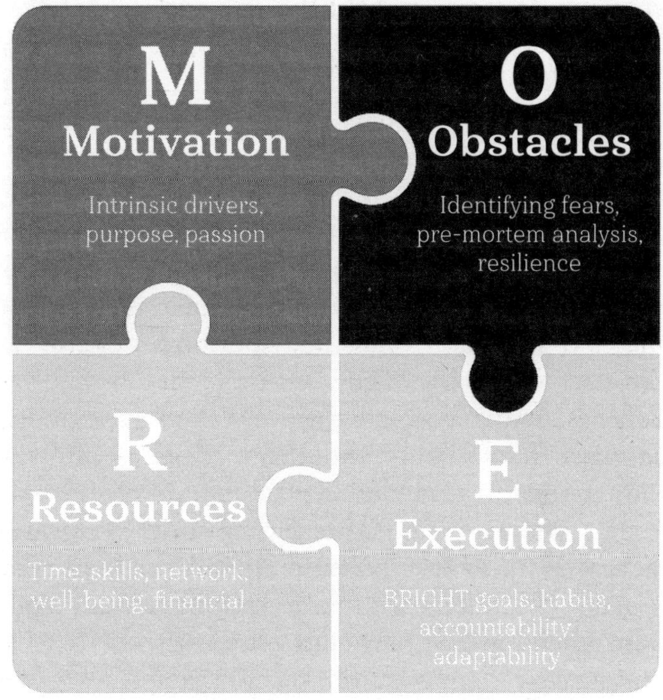

The MORE framework

core **Ikonic Purpose**, consciously fuelling it with unbridled **Passion**, and steadfastly maintaining it through strategic **Persistence** and potent psychological drivers. We're building an inner furnace, not a flickering candle.

If we're brutally honest with ourselves, the external rewards – the bigger car, the applause, the fleeting status symbols – are like sugary snacks. They offer a quick, exhilarating hit, a fantastic feeling in the moment, but they're not sustainable fuel for the long, often challenging, journey to extraordinary success. They simply don't last when the path gets rocky, when the initial excitement wanes or when the grind gets undeniably relentless.

Intrinsic motivation, on the other hand, is the deep, resonant satisfaction that emanates from within. This, my friends, is where the real magic lives. It's the profound difference between climbing a mountain solely for the Instagrammable view from the summit and climbing it because the challenging ascent itself, the act of striving and overcoming, makes every fibre of your being feel exhilaratingly alive.

Explore your intrinsic drivers by asking yourself what work or activities you'd pour your heart and soul into, simply for the joy of doing them. Think about when you feel most authentically you, most alive and engaged. Consider what problems in the world, or in your specific field, ignite a fire within you, making you ache to find solutions and create positive change. Forget external validation for a moment. What personal standards of excellence or mastery truly drive you, even when no one else is watching? That deep-seated drive, that internal compass pointing toward what genuinely lights you up, that's your purpose. And it's the most reliable, high-octane fuel that will keep you tenaciously moving forward when the road inevitably gets tough.

Mastering bulletproof motivation

When I first embarked on my entrepreneurial journey, the idea of financial independence was a powerful external motivator. I had that vision of freedom, autonomy and the ability to create something iconic playing on repeat in my mind. This vision was intrinsically linked to the meaning I sought. The freedom to live by my values, the autonomy to direct my own impact and the legacy I wished to build for my children. But when the late nights stretched into early mornings and the inevitable setbacks and rejections rolled in, it wasn't solely the thought of financial success that kept me going. It was the profound, burning desire to build something truly meaningful, something that would create an Ikonic impact and genuinely help others transform their lives. That's when I fully grasped the enduring, unshakeable power of intrinsic motivation.

Victor Vroom's Expectancy Theory, a cornerstone of motivational psychology developed in 1964, powerfully illuminates this. It posits that our motivation to act is a product of three things. How much we value a particular outcome (Valence), our belief that our efforts will lead to the desired performance (Expectancy) and our belief that successful performance will lead to the valued outcome (Instrumentality). When your BRIGHT goals are aligned with your intrinsic values and you genuinely expect your focused efforts to yield fulfilling results, your motivation doesn't just increase; it skyrockets. You're no longer just chasing external achievements, you're actively pursuing profound fulfilment. It's about forging a sacred contract with your future self, one that you're fiercely, passionately committed to honouring. When your dreams are inextricably tied to your deepest values, you become truly unstoppable. You're not just building a "successful" life by societal standards; you're architecting a life that resonates with the deepest truth of who you are, not who you think you should be.

When your dreams are inextricably tied to your deepest values, you become truly unstoppable

Another key to building this steadfast motivation is to celebrate your small wins with genuine enthusiasm. Every tiny victory, every step forward, releases dopamine in your brain, literally rewiring it for success and reinforcing positive momentum. This concept is rooted in operant conditioning, a psychological principle extensively studied and popularized by B F Skinner. The idea is elegantly simple; behaviours that are followed by positive reinforcement are more likely to be repeated. So, instead of obsessing solely over the distant summit, consciously acknowledge and celebrate every single step forward. That's how you build a powerhouse mindset, one micro-win at a time. For example, during particularly challenging projects, I started meticulously celebrating even the smallest victories – completing a daunting daily checklist, successfully navigating a difficult conversation or reaching a micro-milestone on a project. These tiny celebrations kept me motivated and on track, creating a powerful positive feedback loop that propelled me forward, day after day.

To make this intensely practical for you, take a moment right now. Write down three things that truly ignite your passion and are connected to your current BRIGHT goal (see pages 56–9). Then, identify one micro-win related to that goal that you can achieve today. And then, right now, promise yourself you'll celebrate it. Whether it's a quick victory dance in your office, savouring a cup of your favourite coffee with mindful appreciation, or simply taking a quiet moment to acknowledge your progress and dedication, make it meaningful to you. This is about actively rewiring your mindset to recognize and reward progress, thereby building unstoppable resilience. Your next breakthrough isn't some distant, hazy dream; it's being meticulously built on the solid foundation of today's small wins. Make those wins count. Make them matter.

Your motivation manifesto

1 **My top three intrinsic motivators for** [your BRIGHT goal]
2 **Core value connection:** For each motivation above, identify the core value (e.g., freedom, impact, creativity, growth) it directly fuels.
3 **Impact visualization:** Close your eyes and vividly imagine achieving this goal. How will it positively impact your life? The lives of those around you? The wider world? Write down the feelings and images that arise.

Obstacles: transforming barriers into bridges

But even the most potent intrinsic motivation isn't always enough on its own. It will inevitably ebb and flow, especially when the path gets rough and challenges mount. The secret isn't to try and avoid discomfort; that's an exercise in futility. The key is to proactively build the resilience to push through it. That starts with practising radical self-compassion, treating yourself with the same kindness and understanding you'd offer a dear friend when setbacks happen. It's about reframing failures not as damning indictments of your worth, but as invaluable stepping stones.

Actively challenge those insidious negative narratives that can sabotage your progress. Techniques from Cognitive Behavioral Therapy (CBT) are incredibly effective here, helping you to identify, question and reframe distorted or unhelpful thought patterns. When you inevitably stumble, and you will, because growth demands it, refuse to beat yourself up. Instead, pause, breathe and ask with genuine curiosity, "What invaluable lesson can I extract from this experience?" and "How can I leverage this learning to grow stronger and more effective?" It's about consciously building a mental fortress, an inner citadel of resilience that can withstand any storm.

I learned this lesson the hard way after my second business venture, the Enterprise Vault Membership Club, didn't take off as planned. We had the grand launch party, the VIP guests sipped champagne and we celebrated the bold, innovative ideas that I truly believed would transform my clients' businesses. But a crucial element was missing. The perceived value from the target audience wasn't enough to convert interest into membership at the scale I needed. They didn't join in the numbers anticipated, and I was devastated. It would have been easy to give up right there, to let that perceived failure define me. But instead of surrendering to defeat, I made a conscious choice to dissect every mistake, every misstep, every assumption I'd made. I used that painful experience to refine my approach, to deepen my understanding of my audience and to hone my value proposition. I didn't just learn; I adapted, I evolved and I came back stronger.

Roadblocks on the path to significant achievement are inevitable. The sooner you accept this, anticipate them, and even learn to embrace them, the more powerful you become. Obstacles aren't your enemy; they're your most potent teachers, disguised challenges designed to test your resolve and refine your strategy. The critical difference between those who crumble under pressure and those who conquer adversity lies squarely in their ability to transform setbacks into strategic advantages. Life, and especially the pursuit of meaningful, audacious goals, isn't a smooth, linear path; it's a thrilling, winding road, often filled with unexpected turns, steep climbs and unforeseen detours. These obstacles, these seemingly insurmountable barriers, are precisely where your greatest growth, your deepest learning and your most profound resilience are forged. So, instead of viewing them as problems that halt your progress, learn to embrace them as divine signposts, guiding you to innovate, adapt and, ultimately, forge ahead by turning your barriers into bridges.

Pre-mortem analysis

One of the most powerful proactive strategies is pre-mortem analysis. If, like me, you've experienced plans that have spectacularly failed, this technique offers a radical way to learn from the past to predict and prevent future setbacks. Think of it as possessing a crystal ball that allows you to see potential pitfalls before you even take the first step. Before launching a major project or pursuing a significant goal, gather your team (or do this solo) and ask: "Imagine it's [X date in the future] and this project/goal has failed spectacularly. What went wrong?" Brainstorm every possible reason for failure. By identifying the most likely pitfalls now and building in safeguards or contingency plans, you create a robust backup strategy for problems before they even materialize. This isn't pessimism, it's astute strategic foresight.

When I was preparing to launch my new business, Ikonology, I made a deliberate choice to conduct a thorough pre-mortem analysis. I, along with my core team, envisioned every conceivable way it could falter. Insufficient funding, unexpected market shifts, key team member conflicts, technological failures, stronger-than-anticipated competitor moves. By unflinchingly visualizing these potential disasters, we were able to proactively develop contingency plans and risk-mitigation strategies for each. And when some of those challenges inevitably arose, we were prepared. They didn't take us by surprise; we had already charted a potential path through the storm. This exercise reduces future anxiety and builds present confidence. You're not just vaguely hoping for the best; you're strategically preparing for the worst while simultaneously optimizing for resounding success.

Fear, whether it's the fear of failure, the fear of judgement or even the fear of success itself, can be a powerful paralysing agent on your journey. The first step is to acknowledge it. Name it. Then, challenge it. Fear is often nothing more than a phantom, a powerless illusion that only holds as much sway as you grant it. Here, you can try **exposure therapy**, a technique adapted from the behavioural therapy work of pioneers like Joseph Wolpe. This involves confronting your fears in controlled, manageable and incremental ways. The objective is to systematically desensitize yourself, proving to your nervous system that the feared outcome is either unlikely or manageable. Fear is just a signal, often pointing directly to your growth edge. When I was first starting out, public speaking terrified me. My heart would race, my palms would sweat and I'd often freeze mid-sentence. But instead of avoiding it, I made a conscious decision to face it head-on. I started by speaking to very small, supportive groups, then gradually increased the audience size and the complexity of

When you adopt a growth mindset, you don't just survive setbacks, you actively learn from them the topics. Each time, I proved to myself that I could do it, that I could survive the discomfort, and little by little, the fear began to lose its suffocating grip. Now, public speaking isn't just something I do; it's something I genuinely thrive on, a powerful way to connect and create impact.

Challenges aren't proof of your inadequacy; they're precious opportunities to sharpen your skills and fortify your resolve. A "growth mindset", a concept popularized by Stanford psychologist Carol Dweck in her seminal book *Mindset: The New Psychology of Success* wholeheartedly embraces difficulty as a springboard for development. It's about leaning into failure, viewing it as an essential, non-negotiable step in levelling up your execution game.

Think of your abilities and talents not as fixed, immutable traits, but as malleable, expandable capabilities. When you adopt a growth mindset, you don't just survive setbacks, you actively learn from them. You see them not as definitive roadblocks but as valuable feedback loops, guiding you toward refinement and improvement. Every challenge becomes an invitation to evolve. Instead of shying away, face it head-on with a mindset that declares, "This is making me stronger, wiser and more capable."

Build your resilience blueprint

To turn this powerful insight into practical, actionable progress, use the following journal prompts to outline your resilience strategy:

1. **Identify your biggest fear:** What specific fear is currently holding you back or causing the most resistance as you pursue your BRIGHT goal? Is it a fear of judgement, fear of failure, fear of the unknown, fear of success? Write it down with unflinching honesty and confront it head-on.
2. **Break it down into actionable (exposure) steps:** What are the smallest, most manageable actions you can take to begin facing this fear?

- If it's public speaking: Start by practising your presentation in front of a mirror, then to a trusted friend, then to a small group, gradually increasing the challenge.
- If it's fear of rejection (e.g., in sales): Begin by reaching out to one low-stakes potential client or connection, focusing on the act of outreach itself rather than the outcome.

3 **Challenge your thought patterns (cognitive restructuring):** Fear-based thoughts are not just roadblocks; they are the invisible chains that shackle your potential, keeping you trapped in old patterns and suffocating new opportunities. To shatter these limiting narratives and reclaim your power, this simple yet profound exercise provides a strategic blueprint. By systematically exposing the thoughts that hold you captive, rigorously weighing the evidence, and consciously forging a new perspective, you will transform fear into fuel, stepping forward with resolute clarity and audacious confidence. Let's wield this tool and reframe your reality.

Negative Thought	Evidence Supporting This Thought	Evidence Contradicting This Thought	Empowering Reframe
Example			
I'm going to fail this launch.	My last idea didn't take off as planned.	I've successfully completed complex projects before. I've learnt valuable lessons from the last attempt. I have a better strategy now.	Every attempt is a learning opportunity. I 'm well-prepared and capable of navigating challenges for this launch.

Obstacles aren't immutable barriers; they're opportunities in disguise, invitations to innovate. Transform your mindset to see challenges as pathways to profound growth. Whether it's using pre-mortem analysis to strategically prepare for potential setbacks, systematic exposure therapy to courageously dismantle fear, or consciously cultivating a growth mindset to embrace the climb, every strategy you employ fuels your unstoppable progress. Your next level of success isn't found on a smooth, easy road; it lies just beyond the obstacle you're willing to courageously conquer. Because on the other side of fear, lies your greatest growth. Stop seeing barriers as threats and start seeing them as bridges to your greatness.

On the other side of fear, lies your greatest growth

Resources: fuel your mission

Resources, in the context of achieving your grandest visions, extend far beyond the purely financial. They encompass your unique skills and talents, your supportive network, your invaluable time and, crucially, your vibrant well-being. True, sustainable success is about strategically and efficiently leveraging every asset at your disposal. Let's unlock your hidden wells of potential. Think of these multifaceted resources as the premium raw materials you need to meticulously build your vision. Just as a master architect carefully selects precisely the right materials for a magnificent and enduring structure, you too must identify, cultivate and strategically deploy the resources that will most powerfully support your unique journey.

Your skills

Let's start by identifying the skills absolutely essential for bringing your vision to life. Whether it's dynamic leadership, persuasive marketing, sharp financial literacy or effective communication, commit to a clear, intentional growth plan. Actively take courses, seek out mentors who've achieved what you aspire to, and voraciously invest in expanding your knowledge base. Your potential is genuinely limitless if you're willing to consistently upgrade your personal and professional toolkit. I vividly remember when I realized that my digital marketing skills were significantly holding back the growth of my early ventures. Instead of just accepting this as a limitation, I enrolled in targeted online courses, sought out mentors who were experts in the field and dedicated specific time each week to learning and implementing new strategies. This focused investment in myself paid off tenfold, allowing me to reach a much wider audience and exponentially grow my business.

Your network

One of the most critical, yet often profoundly underestimated, aspects of resource management is the conscious cultivation of your network – your tribe, your circle of influence. This isn't about collecting contacts; it's about intentionally surrounding yourself with your people. For me, these incredible humans are beacons of high, positive energy (absolutely no room for energy vampires or perpetual drama!), individuals who are not just success-driven but also deeply values-aligned. Your environment, the company you keep, profoundly shapes your mindset and your trajectory, so curate it with fierce intentionality and bold standards. This is never about the sheer quantity of connections; it's always about the quality, the resonance and the reciprocal uplift.

Seek out mentors whose wisdom illuminates your path and whose achievements inspire you to stretch beyond your perceived limits. Find peers who don't just agree with you, but who courageously challenge your thinking, spark innovative collaboration, and celebrate your victories as if they were their own. Forge partnerships with those who genuinely elevate your game, pushing you toward your highest potential. Understand this: the people you choose to invest your precious time and energy with have a significant, and often subconscious, impact on your beliefs, your behaviours, your aspirations and, ultimately, the altitude you reach.

Particularly after transitioning from the structured environment of the corporate world, I made a very conscious and deliberate effort to seek out and connect with individuals who genuinely inspired me – those who were already living their version of *More Money, More Life.* I sought out people who consistently challenged me to think bigger, to act bolder, and to step more fully into my own power. These connections, nurtured with authenticity and mutual respect, ultimately formed my new, empowering circle of influence. These relationships became more than just contacts; they were lifelines, providing invaluable support during challenging times, offering fresh, expansive perspectives when I felt stuck, and miraculously opening doors to opportunities and collaborations I wouldn't have discovered, or perhaps even dared to pursue, on my own. Your network is a reflection and a magnifier of your own evolving energy and ambition.

Your time

Your most precious, non-renewable currency is your time. To master it, consider using tools like the Eisenhower Matrix, a simple yet profound framework that helps you categorize tasks based on their urgency and importance. This method, inspired by former US President Dwight D. Eisenhower, assists in prioritizing tasks to enhance productivity and focus. It allows you to ruthlessly prioritize high-impact activities that directly move you toward your BRIGHT goals, strategically delegate low-value tasks that drain your energy or don't leverage your unique genius, automate mundane and repetitive processes wherever possible, and dedicate your prime, focused time only to strategic execution and high-value creation. Time is a finite resource, and its strategic allocation dictates the trajectory of your success. I learned to ruthlessly prioritize, focusing my energy solely on tasks that would yield the greatest impact and align with my core objectives. Anything that didn't meet this high-value threshold was delegated, automated or eliminated, thereby freeing up my mental bandwidth for strategic thinking and decisive, impactful action.

Your well-being

At the very core of your financial success, and indeed your overall life fulfilment, lies a fundamental, non-negotiable truth. You are your most powerful resource. Your mental, emotional and physical well-being aren't just pleasant accessories to achievement; they're the solid foundation upon which everything else is meticulously built. The truth is, without a resilient mind and a strong, vibrant body, your grandest goals remain merely theoretical – lofty ideas lacking the essential energy, clarity and stamina to bring them into tangible reality. Peak performance isn't about pushing harder; it's about intelligently building sustainable habits that consistently recharge, renew and fortify you. When you neglect your well-being, it's akin to attempting to run a high-performance engine on low-quality, contaminated fuel; you might sputter forward for a while, but you'll inevitably break down, often at the most critical junctures.

Prioritize your well-being as if it's your most valuable investment, because it absolutely is

Prioritize your well-being as if it's your most valuable investment, because it absolutely is. Consciously incorporate the essentials – optimal nutrition, consistent movement, restorative sleep and practices for mental clarity (like mindfulness or meditation) – into your daily life, not as optional extras to be squeezed in if time permits, but as non-negotiable priorities. This is about creating routines that energize your body, focus your mind and fortify your spirit, giving you the enduring stamina to pursue greatness without succumbing to burnout.

When I made the conscious decision to prioritize my self-care, it wasn't about indulging in a fleeting wellness trend; it was a profound strategic decision to become truly unstoppable. I made a commitment to regular exercise, choosing activities that not only challenged my body but also invigorated my mind and lifted my spirit. I embraced healthy eating not as a restrictive diet, but as an act of profound self-respect, intentionally nourishing my body with foods that fuelled my performance rather than drained my energy. And I cultivated a consistent mindfulness practice, incorporating daily rituals that kept my mind centred, focused and resilient in the face of challenges. The transformation wasn't just physical, it was deeply mental and emotional. I became sharper, more creative and infinitely more productive. My ideas flowed with greater clarity, and I found myself navigating challenges with a calm, resourceful and focused mindset. Taking care of my well-being wasn't a luxury; it was, and continues to be, an essential, foundational pillar of my success and fulfilment. Self-care is a lifelong, evolving commitment to honouring yourself. It's about creating a lifestyle that consistently amplifies your power rather than draining it. You'll quickly notice that when you prioritize your well-being, everything else in your life begins to flow with greater ease and purpose. You think clearer, act bolder and execute with intention. The best, most leveraged investment you can ever make is in your own resilience – physical, mental and emotional. This is how you build a life where you don't just succeed; you truly, vibrantly thrive.

> Execution is the great separator. It's what distinguishes the perpetual dreamers from the world-changing doers

Your resource inventory & enhancement plan

1 **My top five personal assets:** List the resources – your key skills, most supportive connections/network elements, unique

knowledge and even personal qualities (e.g., resilience, creativity) – that will fuel your goal.

2 **Identify critical gaps & develop an action plan:** Where are your most significant resource weaknesses in relation to your BRIGHT goal? What specific skills, connections or knowledge do you need to acquire or strengthen? Create a mini plan to address one key gap. For example:
   - Gap: lack of advanced digital marketing skills for my online business.
   - Action plan: this month, I'll research and enroll in a reputable online digital marketing course (Budget: £X). I'll dedicate five hours per week to study and implementation. I'll also reach out to [Name of contact] to ask for advice on key strategies.

3 **Daily well-being commitment:** Commit to one small, non-negotiable daily habit that improves your mental or physical health. Choose something you can realistically implement today (e.g., a ten-minute morning walk, five minutes of guided meditation before work, drink two litres of water …).

Execution: where your dreams meet undeniable victory

This is it. The crucible where inspired intention meets decisive, bold action. Execution isn't just about "doing" things; it's about leading with strategic intention. It's the ruthless commitment to relentless consistency, laser-focused effort and steadfast, targeted accountability. It's time to cut through the noise, eliminate distractions and turn your courageous plans into undeniable, tangible progress.

Execution is the great separator. It's what distinguishes the perpetual dreamers from the world-changing doers, the meticulous planners from the high-impact performers. It's the grit to take daily, purposeful action even when motivation temporarily fades, and the unflinching discipline that shatters complacency and forges your lasting legacy.

Firstly, let's go back and revisit our BRIGHT goals (see pages 56–9). Think of yourself as a master sculptor, patiently yet purposefully chiselling away at the marble of your immense potential. Each BRIGHT goal is a precise, intentional stroke that meticulously shapes your masterpiece of success. This framework puts you firmly in the driving seat, making you the conscious architect of your path with ruthless clarity. Break down your grand ambitions into manageable, actionable tasks and track your progress with unwavering diligence.

Example: if your BRIGHT goal is to double your client base within six months and welcome an extra £100,000 into your world, breathe life into it. Let purpose, poetry and heart guide every step:

- **Bold:** Invite two dream clients each month – souls who reflect your highest vision. Approach with courage, and let strategic partnerships open gateways to new circles of transformation.
- **Reachable:** Turn consistency into ritual: 20 personalized invitations sent weekly, each infused with value and intention. Honour the yes, respect the no, and let data quietly guide your refinement with every response.
- **Inspiring:** Light a beacon. Gather the voices of those whose journeys you've transformed, weaving their stories into living testimonies – windows of possibility for those still searching.
- **Genuine:** Work only with those whose essence resonates with yours. Let connection always eclipse transaction, creating a tapestry of relationships that deepen and strengthen over time.
- **Heartfelt:** Let every message be a love letter to your mission. Thread empathy, gratitude and care through every interaction. Celebrate your clients' wins as your own, and let kindness become the melody of your brand.

- **Transformative:** Welcome clients as family. Design onboarding as an experience of delight – a cascade of thoughtful gestures and unexpected value. Watch as satisfied clients become joyful storytellers, carrying your message further than you imagined.

Every BRIGHT goal is a sacred invitation – not just to tally numbers, but to lead with vision, serve with heart, and transform your work into meaning, legacy and impact.

The alchemy of habit

Habits are the invisible architecture of your identity. They're the often-unconscious daily rituals that incrementally define who you're becoming and ultimately determine the magnitude of your success. It's the small, seemingly insignificant, consistent actions that compound over time to produce extraordinary results.

To automate your triumph, consciously build consistent habits that directly support your BRIGHT goals. To break the powerful inertia of starting something new or challenging, embrace the **Two-Minute Rule**, a brilliantly simple yet profoundly effective tool popularized by James Clear in his bestselling book *Atomic Habits.* This rule is all about scaling down your new desired habit to a version that takes absolutely no more than two minutes to do. Instead of aiming for an hour-long, intense workout, commit to doing just two minutes of focused exercise (like ten push-ups or a two-minute plank). Instead of feeling overwhelmed by the thought of writing a whole chapter, commit to writing just two compelling sentences.

The objective isn't to achieve monumental results in those initial two minutes; it's to make the act of starting the habit as effortless and non-intimidating as possible. This systematically removes the mental barrier of resistance and makes it almost ridiculously easy to begin. Consistency is the golden key here; the most important thing is to show up and do the two-minute version of the habit every single day, without fail. This diligently establishes the routine and begins to build positive momentum. Once the two-minute habit is ingrained and feels automatic, you can then gradually, almost imperceptibly, increase the duration or intensity. The key is to make progress in small, sustainable and confidence-boosting steps. This rule works so effectively because it overcomes resistance by making the habit feel less daunting, thereby significantly reducing procrastination. It also helps you to shift your identity, as you start to see yourself as someone who does the habit (e.g., "I'm someone who exercises daily", "I'm a writer who writes every day"). And finally, it creates powerful momentum, because it's always easier to continue an action once you've started, even if that start was just for two minutes.

From these small, consistent actions, your desired identity and extraordinary results will emerge. Just as a tiny stream can eventually carve a grand canyon, your two-minute habits, compounded over time, will sculpt the reality of your BRIGHT goals.

Accountability and adaptability

Accountability is the cornerstone of high-level execution. It's the often uncomfortable but absolutely essential bridge that spans the divide between hollow intentions and undeniable, tangible results. Find an accountability partner – a trusted coach, a dedicated mentor or a supportive peer, who not only believes in your vision but also holds you to a higher standard of performance. This should be someone who sees your limitless potential even when temporary doubt clouds your own vision. It should be a strategic alliance forged in the shared fire of ambition and mutual respect.

Track your progress with ruthless precision. Celebrate every victory, no matter how small, because these wins are the essential fuel for your sustained fire. Build a system that actively rewards relentless, focused action and makes inertia uncomfortable. It's about owning your legacy, one intentional day at a time. You're not just holding yourself accountable to a to-do list; you're holding yourself accountable to your grand vision, your untapped potential and the magnificent future self that is eagerly waiting to be unleashed.

Plans will inevitably encounter unexpected turbulence. Life will unleash its fury in the form of unforeseen challenges and market shifts. In this dynamic landscape, adaptability isn't just a desirable skill, it's your crucial tactical edge and your most potent weapon against chaos and uncertainty. It's your inherent ability to pivot with lethal precision, to recalibrate your approach with ruthless efficiency when circumstances demand it. True execution isn't about rigidly clinging to a sinking ship of outdated plans; it's about courageously navigating the storm with a resolute vision and relentless agility. Regularly and honestly dissect your progress, courageously expose inefficiencies or misalignments, and then strike fearlessly and decisively into the heart of necessary change.

Conquering procrastination

Procrastination isn't a simple character flaw, it's a complex mental siege; a fortress often built upon foundations of fear (of failure, of success, of judgement) and overwhelm. It's a maladaptive coping mechanism to avoid negative emotions associated with a task. The temporary relief we get from putting something off reinforces the avoidance behaviour, even though it ultimately creates more stress and hinders progress. To breach its formidable walls, you need to launch a full-scale, strategic assault on its root causes. You're not just fighting procrastination, you're going to obliterate it, and here's how:

Progress, however small, breeds further progress

Deploy the **Pomodoro Technique** like a series of precision strikes. This time-management method, developed by Francesco Cirillo, involves breaking your work into focused 25-minute intervals (called "pomodoros") separated by short breaks. When you dismantle a daunting, monolithic task into these rapid, manageable skirmishes, momentum becomes almost inevitable. You're not tackling the entire mountain in one go; you're conquering it one fierce, focused step at a time.

Unfinished tasks aren't just loose ends; they often feel like mental landmines, generating what psychologists call cognitive tension and insidiously sapping your precious energy. Use the **Zeigarnik Effect** to your advantage. This psychological phenomenon, named after Bluma Zeigarnik, describes how our brains tend to remember uncompleted or interrupted tasks better than completed ones, creating a persistent urge for closure. You can leverage this by simply starting a task, even if you only work on it for a few minutes. That act of initiation plants the seed in your subconscious, creating that gentle internal nudge to return and complete it. Launch swift, even imperfect, offensives on your tasks to clear mental space and reclaim your focus. Start the task, even if it's messy. Just get it moving. Progress, however small, breeds further progress.

Motivation flickers, but purpose burns with an infernal, unquenchable intensity. Anchor every single action, every daily task, to your strategic imperative – the bigger, more meaningful "why" behind your grind. Purpose isn't a fleeting spark; it's a raging wildfire that will keep you moving forward with conviction, even when motivation temporarily fades. Get brutally clear on why achieving this goal truly matters to you, and consciously feed that fire daily with affirmations, visualizations and reminders of your vision.

By mastering the MORE framework, by intentionally cultivating your **Motivation**, strategically navigating **Obstacles**, optimally leveraging your **Resources**, and committing to relentless **Execution,** you're forging a strategic path toward extraordinary achievement. Dream with unbridled ambition. Act with surgical, ruthless precision. And remember, profound success doesn't merely come to those who yearn for it; it's seized, with your determination, and by those who dare to execute with indomitable force.

CHAPTER 8
PROTECTING YOUR LEGACY

"Someday" is the insidious disease that will silently carry your dreams to the grave.

– Tim Ferriss

Life's grand symphony crescendos with a universal truth. Money, opportunity and even love are most readily captured by those who embrace speed and decisiveness. The swift, exhilarating breeze of possibility whispers most audibly to those poised to act, to those who dare to seize fleeting moments and courageously mould them into their destiny. In this dynamic dance with fortune, wealth and impact gravitate toward those who master the art of intentional, timely action. As you embark on your financial odyssey, remember this; fortune truly favours the bold, the ready, the swift.

But building wealth is not a solitary conquest of accumulation; it's a profound dual mandate of creation and conscientious preservation. It's not enough to construct a magnificent financial fortress; you must also ensure its strength endures, sheltering and empowering those you cherish long after your own chapter closes. This chapter is dedicated to illuminating the essential tools for this vital task

Protecting your legacy means crafting a financial story that transcends your lifetime, leaving behind a narrative of support, sustainability and love

– wills, trusts, and powers of attorney – with crystal clarity. Our goal is to transform these intimidating legal concepts from sources of confusion into potent instruments of your empowerment. Protecting your legacy means crafting a financial story that transcends your lifetime, leaving behind a narrative of support, sustainability and love for your loved ones, not a burden of unforeseen chaos and distress.

A lesson forged in pain

The vital importance of having your financial house in impeccable order isn't just an abstract concept to me; it's a visceral lesson etched deep into my soul, forged in the brutal crucible of personal experience. My father, a man whose laughter could illuminate any room, whose boundless spirit and generosity knew no limits, tragically left behind a legacy tainted by financial chaos, a heavy shadow that loomed over our lives long after he was gone.

He was the vibrant life of every gathering. The first to extend a hand in friendship, to buy the next round at the bar, to share a story that left everyone doubled over with laughter. His philosophy was simple but powerful: "Be generous with your friends. Share your joy, your laughter and your brass (money), because life's about sticking together."

That generosity, vibrant spirit, cheeky sense of fun and his solid faith in the inherent good of people, is the beautiful legacy I choose to carry with me. It's a flame that both warms my heart with cherished memories and constantly challenges me to be better, to honour his spirit while learning from the pain of his financial mistakes. It's a daily reminder of the delicate, crucial balance between a generous heart and a responsible, proactive hand. And while it's not always a balance I get perfectly right, I strive to embody it every single day.

In my dad's final months, a disquieting shift occurred. His boisterous laughter began to fade, the familiar social gatherings dwindled, and our conversations, while deepening, took on an unfamiliar weight. We started venturing into uncharted emotional territories, and I sensed that something was profoundly amiss. He spoke of not wanting people to be maudlin over his grave, a cryptic foreshadowing of the turmoil that lay hidden beneath the surface.

Unbeknown to me, his world was unravelling with terrifying speed. A monumental project, one into which he'd poured his heart, soul and years of effort, teetered on the brink of collapse. A relentless tide of financial pressures began to engulf him: mortgage arrears mounting, credit card debt spiralling out of control, overdrafts looming like hungry shadows. The last time I saw him, I was rushing, late again, caught in the chaos of another trading floor crisis at Goldman Sachs that refused to wait. When we did finally meet that evening, he spoke of life, of his growing weariness, but I remained tragically oblivious to the true magnitude of his struggle. As I cycled away through the bustling London traffic, I had no inkling that it would be our final farewell. A week later, a massive heart attack silenced his vibrant voice forever. The crushing weight of unspoken financial pressure had proved too heavy a burden for even his indomitable spirit to bear.

The ripple effect of unspoken financial chaos

The aftermath was a brutal awakening, a stark confrontation with a reality we were utterly unprepared for. We arrived at his house to find the front entrance barricaded by a mountain of unopened mail. Demand letters and final notices a chilling testament to months, perhaps years, of silent desperation. The stark truth hit us like a physical blow; selling everything he owned wouldn't even begin to extinguish the flames of his debt. We were forced to declare him bankrupt, a final indignity that would have mortified my proud, generous father.

Financial disarray doesn't merely deplete your bank account; it erodes your peace of mind, fractures your relationships and casts a long, dark shadow over your legacy. This truth is powerfully illustrated by Erik Erikson's psycho-social theory of development, specifically the stage of "Generativity vs. Stagnation". In Erikson's framework, this is a crucial stage in adulthood where individuals grapple with the fundamental question, "Have I made my mark? Have I contributed something meaningful that will outlast me?" Generativity, the positive resolution of this stage, involves finding profound meaning and fulfilment in contributing to the world beyond oneself – through raising a family, creating something of lasting value in their work, mentoring others or contributing to the betterment of society. It's about leaving a positive imprint, a legacy of care, creation and contribution.

Stagnation, on the other hand, represents the negative outcome. It's characterized by a sense of self-absorption, a lack of purpose and a gnawing feeling of having made no real, lasting contribution. When financial disarray defines a person's life, it can severely hinder their ability to achieve generativity. Instead of focusing on leaving a positive mark, their energy becomes consumed by their own struggles, often leaving behind a legacy of chaos, confusion and emotional burden for their loved ones. Your legacy, therefore, isn't just about the wealth you accumulate; it's about the emotional wake you leave behind. It's the stories your loved ones tell, the peace or turmoil you bequeath. Did you create a foundation for future generations to build upon, or did you leave them to navigate the wreckage? The answer to that question defines the true value and resonance of your legacy.

Joe Vitale, a guiding voice in the world of the Law of Attraction, reminds us that speed isn't reckless haste; it's a vital catalyst for manifestation. His concept of the "Attractor Factor" underscores the principle that aligning your actions with clear, powerful intentions accelerates the process of attracting financial success and shaping your desired legacy.

Imagine a musical note. Intention is the purity of the note itself, clear, focused and resonant. Action is the speed and consistency with which that note vibrates. A note sounded with strong, clear intention, vibrating rapidly and consistently, will travel further, resonate more powerfully and have a far greater impact than a sluggish, muddled or hesitant sound. That's the power of aligned, decisive action.

In my dad's story, the tragedy wasn't a lack of good intention – he was a proud and generous man – but a lack of swift, decisive action in managing his financial affairs. Opportunities to address the mounting debt, to seek help, to put his affairs in order were tragically missed. The "vibration" of his financial life, instead of resonating with strength and clarity, became a slow, chaotic hum that ultimately overwhelmed him.

This book, then, is part of his legacy, transformed. It's a story of how his financial trauma can become a powerful lesson, a catalyst to help you and others move from financial chaos to empowering clarity. It's about transforming a personal tragedy into a roadmap for collective healing and financial empowerment. This isn't about acting on impulse; it's about moving with clarity, focused intention and the courage to act when opportunities – to organize, to protect, to communicate, to simplify – align with your long-term vision for your life and legacy. It's about recognizing that inaction also has a vibrational frequency, one of stagnation, missed potential and unintended negative consequences.

Ultimately, strategic speed and decisiveness are essential to both wealth creation and the crafting of an enduring, positive legacy. Cultivate the courage to take swift, deliberate action when those crucial opportunities present themselves; be it the opportunity to finally draft that will, to have that difficult but necessary conversation with family, or to simplify and organize your financial affairs. Discern between fleeting distractions and strategic imperatives, and stay strongly aligned with your long-term vision. Don't wait for the mythical "perfect moment". Create it here and now, with the choices you make and the intention you bring to each day. It's in those moments of decisive action that we not only shape our financial destinies but also lay the foundation for a legacy that resonates with purpose, strength and enduring love, echoing meaningfully through generations to come.

Why building wealth isn't enough

We're the architects of ascent, often relentlessly climbing toward our definitions of financial success. We strategize, we hustle, we build our empires of wealth, brick by painstaking brick. Yet, a dangerous illusion can take hold – the seductive belief that wealth, once attained, is a self-sustaining force, an invincible fortress impregnable against the erosion of time and circumstance. This is the paradox of accumulation. We pour our life energy into acquiring wealth, yet often neglect the crucial art of preserving and protecting it, leaving our hard-won fortunes vulnerable to the unpredictable whims of fate. It's like meticulously constructing a magnificent sandcastle, an awe-inspiring testament to our skill and ambition, only to watch the inexorable tide creep in and erode its foundations, grain by grain, until all that remains is a memory and the sting of preventable loss.

Why does this happen? Why do even the most intelligent and driven individuals sometimes fall into this trap? It's often rooted in two powerful, conflicting forces – optimism and denial. We're naturally wired to envision our success as permanent, because the alternative, the thought that everything we've built could crumble, is often too terrifying to fully confront. This idea can be so overwhelming that our minds may subconsciously block it out. We can become attached to a static view of wealth, believing it fixed and immovable,

We pour our life energy into acquiring wealth, yet often neglect the crucial art of preserving and protecting it because acknowledging its inherent fragility feels like inviting catastrophe.

This illusion of permanence, this seductive song of invincibility, can lull us into complacency. We cling to the comforting notion that our wealth is a static entity, a fixed point in an ever-shifting universe, forgetting that the world is a relentless force of change, a constant dance of creation and destruction. Markets fluctuate, economies transform, laws evolve and unforeseen personal events can shatter even the most meticulously laid plans.

Warren Buffett, a voice of profound financial wisdom, masterfully understands this fundamental truth. He famously speaks of businesses needing a strong competitive "moat" to protect their long-term value from competitors. This principle applies directly to our personal wealth and legacy. Just as a company's advantage can be eroded over time by disruptive innovation or shifting market trends, our hard-earned personal wealth isn't invincible either. It constantly faces potential erosion from forces such as inflation silently diminishing its purchasing power, the inevitable impact of taxes, unexpected economic downturns, unforeseen liabilities or simply our own lack of proactive management. Complacency is the enemy of enduring wealth. Therefore, to truly safeguard our legacy and ensure our financial fortress stands strong for generations, we must adopt a mindset of perpetual vigilance. This means consciously and consistently reinforcing our financial defences, anticipating potential threats, and intelligently diversifying our risks. Not just across different types of financial assets, but across the very fabric of our lives and future plans. This proactive stance isn't about fear; it's about wisdom, foresight and the empowered commitment to protecting what we build.

Complacency is the enemy of enduring wealth

Resistance to the natural flow of wealth management, which includes planning for preservation, creates blockages that hinder continued growth and protection. When we cling too tightly to what we've accumulated and resist the proactive steps of organizing and safeguarding, we can inadvertently disrupt the very forces that enabled us to build that wealth in the first place. Wealth, like life itself, is a dynamic process, a constant exchange of energy. To preserve it effectively, we must remain in a state of fluid, informed action. Adapting to change, seizing opportunities for protection and releasing outdated approaches that no longer serve us.

Lessons from the financial titans

I witnessed the devastating impact of this complacency firsthand during my time at Morgan Stanley, particularly when the 2008 financial crisis erupted, with the collapse of Lehman Brothers serving as a stark epicentre. In the years leading up to its downfall, Lehman was a Wall Street titan, a seemingly invincible financial powerhouse. Some of my friends and colleagues who worked there were brilliant, driven and had amassed fortunes most could only dream of. Yet, despite their remarkable intellect and financial acumen, many fell prey to the illusion of permanence, believing their individual success and the institution's stability were unassailable. This, for some, led to very tough financial times.

It wasn't just Lehman Brothers as an entity that crumbled; it was the individual belief systems of many who thought their wealth was secure simply by being associated with such a powerful name. Some became complacent, perhaps overleveraged in their personal finances, or blind to the systemic risks lurking beneath the surface of the booming market. When the crisis struck, Lehman's carefully constructed empire collapsed within days, leaving many individuals, not just its top executives, facing not only financial losses but also profound uncertainty and a shattering of their perceived security. Their downfall serves as a chilling reminder that even the most formidable fortunes or successful careers can be vulnerable if not underpinned by vigilant, adaptable and personal protective strategies.

You may have conquered worlds, amassed fortunes or built a successful career, yet the ticking clock of life and its inherent uncertainties can remain a blind spot. Perhaps it's a subtle belief in your own exemption, a feeling that "it won't happen to me", that you're somehow beyond the common fate. The intense drive that fuelled your success, while powerful, can sometimes eclipse the wisdom of long-view planning. Our culture often whispers of endless possibility, and the world of finance promotes relentless growth, but the fundamental truths of life, including its eventual end and the certainty of taxes, are inevitable. Ignoring this, even unintentionally, puts your hard-earned legacy at risk. So, consider the long game of preservation not as a morbid preoccupation or a defeat, but as the ultimate act of responsible victory and enduring love.

The tools of wealth preservation

I've worked with countless women who've come from incredibly challenging socioeconomic backgrounds but, despite all the odds, have built not just personal wealth but also pathways to generational security for their families. What unites them isn't just their drive or ambition; it's their mindset. They don't just focus on accumulation, they commit to preservation and intentional legacy. They move beyond mere acquisition to create financial plans that reflect their highest aspirations and deepest values.

They embody "aligned action". They are decisive, proactive and committed to building wealth that endures. It's not about clinging fearfully to what they've achieved, but about continuously reinforcing their foundations and evolving their strategies. They understand that building wealth is only half the battle; the other half is protecting it, nurturing it and positioning it to withstand the tests of time and circumstance.

These women are the true architects of legacy, guided by an intrinsic value system that transcends the mere pursuit of wealth. Their actions aren't driven by fear or greed, but by a profound sense of purpose and a desire to create a positive, lasting impact. Their legacies aren't measured solely by the size of their fortunes, but by the strength of their character, the wisdom they impart and the values they pass on. It's time we all challenge the illusion of permanence and embrace a more resilient, adaptive approach to wealth – one that honours the journey of accumulation while diligently safeguarding the legacy that follows. Wealth is not static, it's a dynamic, living entity that requires constant vigilance, strategic planning and a mindset rooted in both pragmatism and purpose. The climb doesn't end once we reach the summit; it's what we do next that determines whether our legacy stands the test of time or fades like a sandcastle swept away by the tide.

Estate planning is a phrase that can sound like it belongs in a dusty, inaccessible law office, buried under a mountain of jargon and incomprehensible legalese. But at its core, estate planning isn't about arcane bureaucracy or begrudgingly ticking boxes. It's about building an enduring legacy, an unbreakable bridge between your story, your life's work and the future you envision for those you love and the causes you cherish.

It's easy to perceive it as a bewildering maze of wills, trusts and power-of-attorney documents designed more to confuse than to clarify. But the reality is that these are the essential tools with which we sculpt our legacy, the very architecture of lasting security and heartfelt continuity. So, let's break it down, strip away the mystique and transform these potentially intimidating instruments into sources of profound empowerment and peace of mind.

Your will

A will is often an afterthought, a grim, uncomfortable task we instinctively push to the back of our minds. We might treat it like an insurance policy for the inevitable, something to deal with "someday", but thinking of a will in that limited way completely misses its true significance and power. A will isn't just a document of death; it's a vibrant declaration of your life, a powerful expression of your values, your love and your deepest intentions. It's your final, poignant opportunity to shape the narrative of your existence and ensure your legacy lives on through the people and causes that matter most to you.

The weight of this truth crashed into me with the force of a tidal wave when I became pregnant with my first daughter. Suddenly, the world shifted on its axis. It wasn't just about my life anymore; it was about hers, this tiny, precious being who was utterly dependent on me and my husband. A primal instinct to protect, to provide, surged through me. What if something happened to us? Who would ensure she was safe, that she thrived and that she knew the depth of our love? Would she be cared for according to our values, surrounded by the people who cherished her? Would she have the resources to pursue her dreams, to build a life filled with opportunity and joy? The questions were relentless, each one a hammer blow to my heart.

In the midst of that swirling vortex of anxiety and fierce protectiveness, the will emerged. Not as a morbid necessity, but as a lifeline, a powerful tool to extend my love and safeguard her future. It became the vehicle for my most profound hopes, my most fervent wishes. It was the way I could speak, even in silence, to ensure her well-being, to shield her from uncertainty, to guarantee that her inheritance wasn't just financial, but also emotional – a legacy of love and clear intention. I certainly wasn't going to leave her future to the whims of fate, or to the potential influence of those who didn't share our values.

Think of a will as your final love letter, a tangible representation of your desires, crafted with care to protect those you hold dear

Think of a will as your final love letter, a tangible, physical representation of your desires, crafted with care to protect those you hold dear. It eliminates ambiguity, minimizes the potential for conflict and ensures your intentions are understood, loud and clear. It's the ultimate expression of clarity and purpose, a roadmap for your legacy that speaks volumes long after you're gone. It's a way to say, "I love you. I thought of you. I planned for you."

The alternative, the absence of a will, is a silence that speaks volumes. It's a failure to communicate, a void where your guiding voice should be. And that silence can be deafening, creating a vacuum that is often filled with confusion, conflict and unnecessary heartache for those left behind. I wanted to leave nothing to chance, to remove any possibility of confusion or misinterpretation. I wanted to provide my daughter with a sense of security, a foundation of stability upon which she could build her own life, free from the burden of uncertainty and the potential for familial strife. This was of paramount importance to me.

The absence of a will, the act of procrastination, isn't a neutral act; it's a decision by default, a surrender of your control to the impersonal and often unpredictable dictates of the legal system. It's a failure to recognize the profound psychological need for order, for completion, and for the sense of a life well-lived, a story with a defined and considered ending. When we delay creating a will, we leave our loved ones vulnerable, exposed to the potential for conflict, confusion and even financial hardship.

The consequences of this inaction can be devastating, as I witnessed firsthand in the aftermath of my father's passing. We weren't just dealing with grief; we were thrust into a chaotic vortex of legal complexities and family discord. A mountain of paperwork, much of it outdated and conflicting, painted a stark picture of a life in disarray. Divorce decrees hadn't been updated, trusts were still held in marital names and a tangled web of financial loose ends threatened to unravel everything he'd built. What should have been a time for mourning and remembrance became a battleground. A protracted legal struggle that dragged on for years, tearing our family apart, squandering a significant portion of his estate on exorbitant legal fees, and obscuring his true legacy in a fog of bitterness and acrimony. My father, a man who had literally built a whole new village with hundreds of new homes in South Yorkshire, England, whose entrepreneurial spirit had touched countless lives, became, in the end, a casualty of his own financial disorganization. The absence of his voice, his clear, loving instructions, robbed us of the peace and closure we so desperately needed.

When someone dies without a will, they die "intestate", and the law steps in to determine how their assets are divided. This impersonal, bureaucratic process, governed by the rules of intestacy, can have heartbreaking consequences. The rules vary globally, but the core principles are largely consistent: the state, not the individual, dictates the distribution of their estate. Typically, this prioritizes a surviving spouse or civil partner, followed by children and then other relatives (parents, siblings, etc.). This means that a long-term cohabiting partner, no matter how close, may receive nothing automatically; children from a previous relationship could inherit, potentially complicating family dynamics; and estranged family members, with whom the deceased had little or no contact, may inherit before close friends or chosen family. The deceased loses all control over who inherits their assets. Their wishes, values and specific intentions become irrelevant.

If parents die without a will, the court will decide who becomes the legal guardian of any minor children. This decision may not align with the parents' preferences, potentially placing children in the care of someone they didn't want. Dealing with an intestate estate is also often far more complex and time-consuming than dealing with one where a valid will exists. This is because someone must apply to the court for "letters of administration" to manage the estate, which can be a lengthy process; tracing and identifying all potential heirs can be complicated, especially with complex family situations; and the increased complexity can lead to higher legal fees and administrative costs, reducing the value of the estate that ultimately passes to beneficiaries.

The lack of a will isn't just a logistical oversight; it's a profound failure to complete the story of your life with your own authentic voice. It's surrendering your narrative, leaving the final chapter to be written by strangers who don't understand your relationships, your values or your deepest intentions. That's not just a mistake, it's a missed opportunity to ensure your voice is heard, your love is felt and your protection extends even after you're gone.

Now let's touch on how you can take this empowering step to make your will. Don't let intimidation stop you.

Where do you go? You have several options. You can consult a solicitor or an attorney specializing in estate planning. This is often the best route for complex situations or if you want personalized legal advice. There are also reputable online will-writing services that can be very cost-effective and straightforward for simpler estates. Some charities even offer free will-writing services (often in the hope you'll leave them a bequest).

Does it cost anything? Yes, there's typically a cost involved, but it varies hugely. A solicitor will charge more than an online service. Think of it as an investment in peace of mind for you and protection for your loved ones, often far less than the potential legal fees and emotional turmoil of dying intestate. Some online services can be very affordable, sometimes under £100, while a solicitor-drafted will might range from a few hundred to several thousand pounds depending on complexity.

What can you expect from this document? At its core, a will is more than a legal formality, it's a declaration of intent, a final act of agency that ensures your values and your voice endure beyond your lifetime. It names the people you trust most, your executors – the ones who will carry the responsibility of honouring your wishes and managing your estate when you're no longer here to do so yourself. It defines your beneficiaries – those individuals or organizations who will inherit not just your assets, but a piece of your legacy. It allows you to make specific gifts – personal items, cherished heirlooms or financial sums, each one a symbolic gesture of love, gratitude or remembrance.

For parents, it carries even greater weight, allowing you to name guardians for your minor children, ensuring that if the unimaginable were to happen, your children would be cared for by someone you chose, not someone the courts decide. You can also express your funeral preferences. While not always legally binding, these wishes offer clarity and comfort to those left behind. The process itself invites deep reflection, an honest accounting of your assets, your debts and what truly matters. Once drafted, it must be witnessed correctly – a step that's crucial for its validity – and stored in a place that's both secure and accessible. This is not just paperwork, it's a powerful tool of legacy, clarity and peace.

This is not just paperwork, it's a powerful tool of legacy, clarity and peace

Drafting a will is how you ensure your hard work, your life's energy, lives on, not just as financial security, but as a powerful and enduring testament to your vision, your values and your solid commitment to the people and causes that matter most. It's the ultimate act of self-determination, a final declaration of how you want your story to be told, and the impact you want to have on the world. It's about writing the final chapter of your story with your own hand, in your own voice, leaving behind a legacy of love and clarity, not a legacy of loss and confusion.

Writing your legacy letter

Now we move beyond the essential structure of the will itself to capture its very soul. While the will dictates the "what" – the distribution of assets, the appointment of guardians – this exercise helps you articulate the "why". This is your chance to ensure your authentic voice, filled with your love, wisdom and intentions, resonates long after you're gone. This legacy letter is the companion to your will; it's where the heart speaks directly, transforming legal planning into a final, powerful act of connection and enduring love. Let's step into this space of reflection and craft the messages only you can deliver.

Important Note: This letter is a personal expression of love, values and intentions. It's not a legally binding document and doesn't replace or alter your official will. Its purpose is emotional clarity and connection.

Instructions: Use this template as a guide. Adapt it, change it, ignore parts that don't resonate, and add whatever feels authentic to you and your relationship with the recipient. You might write one comprehensive letter or several shorter, more personalized ones. Write from the heart – that's its true power.

To my dearest [Recipient's Name(s)],

As you read this, please know it comes directly from my heart, written with love and deep reflection during my life. While my formal will outlines my wishes for the assets I've accumulated, this letter is about sharing the thoughts, feelings and hopes that truly matter to me, especially concerning you.

Section 1: Expressions of love & gratitude (Choose prompts that fit)

- I want you to know, above all else, how much I love/appreciate/cherish [mention specific qualities of your relationship].

- Thank you for [mention specific joys, support or experiences they brought to your life. Be specific! e.g., "Thank you for your unwavering support during …", "Thank you for the laughter we shared over …", "Thank you for teaching me …"].
- Some of my most treasured memories with you include [share one to three brief, specific memories that highlight your bond].
- I am so proud of you for [mention specific achievements, character traits or ways they live their life].

Section 2: Sharing my values & intentions (Connect to your will if appropriate, gently)

- As I planned for the future and drafted my will, certain values were deeply important to me, such as [mention key values, e.g., fairness, opportunity, security, family harmony, supporting causes I believe in, education, independence].
- My hope in making the decisions I did was to [explain your core intention: e.g., provide a measure of security, give you a head start, honour a promise, ensure fairness as I see it, support your passions].
- Optional (Use with care): Regarding [mention a specific decision or gift, e.g., the house, a sum of money, a specific heirloom], my intention was [explain the "why" from a place of love/value, e.g., "… because I know how much stability means to you", "… to help you pursue your education", "… as a symbol of our shared history"].
- I always believed in the importance of [share a core belief or principle that guided you].

Section 3: Hopes for your future

- My deepest hope for you is that you live a life filled with [e.g., joy, purpose, love, adventure, peace, learning].
- I encourage you to [offer gentle encouragement or advice: e.g., pursue your dreams, be kind to others, never stop learning, take calculated risks, cherish your relationships].

- Remember the importance of [mention things you hope they carry forward, e.g., family connection, integrity, resilience, laughter].
- Don't be afraid to [e.g., make mistakes, ask for help, chart your own course].

Section 4: Life lessons & reflections

- If there's one lesson life taught me that I want to share, it's [share a key piece of wisdom].
- Looking back, I learned the value of [share a reflection on what truly mattered].

Section 5: Closing thoughts

- Please know that my love and belief in you are constants that extend beyond my physical presence.
- Live fully, love deeply and be true to yourself.
- [Add any final personal messages, inside jokes, or affirmations].

With all my love,
(Your Name)
(Date)

Your power of attorney

I know you've worked your butt off to build your life, your wealth and your legacy. But here's a question no one wants to think about. What happens if, one day, you're suddenly unable to manage your own affairs? An unexpected accident. A sudden illness. Cognitive decline creeping in. It's not just a scary thought; for many, it becomes a reality. And if you're not prepared, it can throw your entire life, and the lives of your loved ones, into chaos.

That's where a power of attorney (POA) comes in. Think of it as your ultimate backup plan, your personal contingency strategy. It's the legal document that grants someone you trust (your "attorney" or "agent") the authority to make crucial decisions on your behalf when you can't. This could cover anything from paying bills and managing investments to making critical healthcare choices, depending on the type of POA you set up. It's not about giving up control; paradoxically, it's about keeping control, ensuring your wishes are followed even when you're unable to voice them, no matter what life throws at you. While wills and trusts primarily handle the "after you're gone" side of things, a POA is your vital lifeline while you're still here. It's your voice when you can't speak, your command when you can't act and your clear plan when life goes unexpectedly off script.

If you're the kind of person who thinks ahead, who architects your destiny rather than leaving it to chance, then establishing a power of attorney isn't just advisable, it's your non-negotiable power move. Setting up a POA isn't merely responsible; it's profoundly smart. It's your strategy for protecting your hard-earned interests, safeguarding your wealth and securing your precious peace of mind, ensuring your wishes are honoured whether you face a temporary setback or a more significant, long-term change in capacity.

Taking action now means aligning yourself with empowerment and foresight, setting up your life so that no matter what happens, your affairs can be managed according to your wishes. It's about staying in the driver's seat of your life and keeping the energy flowing positively, even if, for a time, you're not the one physically turning the wheel. If you're still not convinced, imagine this. A self-made entrepreneur in their 40s, a powerhouse of independence and strategy, suffers a severe aneurysm. They're rushed to the hospital, unconscious and fighting for their life. There's no POA in place. Their spouse, who has always relied on them for financial decisions, suddenly finds themselves locked out of joint bank accounts (or unable to access accounts solely in the entrepreneur's name), unable to pay critical business bills or personal mortgage payments, or make urgent decisions for the company. Everything grinds to a halt, while their loved one fights to survive. The stress would be unbearable, yet this level of chaos is completely preventable. A simple POA would have ensured that their spouse could step in without hesitation, protecting the family's financial stability while focusing on what truly matters – recovery and healing.

And it doesn't stop there. Think about aging parents. As dementia or other cognitive challenges set in, they may lose the capacity to make sound decisions about their finances or healthcare. Without a POA, their adult children could face a lengthy, emotionally draining and expensive legal battle to apply to the Court of Protection (in the UK, or a similar process elsewhere) to become a "deputy" or "guardian/conservator". This process can drain energy, finances and emotional bandwidth. In worst-case scenarios, it can even pitch family members against each other, ripping relationships apart. A proactive POA doesn't just avoid legal red tape, it preserves family harmony and ensures that your loved ones are empowered to act swiftly and smoothly in your best interests when you no longer can.

These stories aren't meant to scare you; they're meant to wake you up to the power you have now to protect your future self and your family. A power of attorney is a necessity in our complex world. It's how you protect your wealth, your legacy and the people you care about most. It's about taking charge of your future and safeguarding your hard work, no matter what life throws your way.

So, how does it work, and how do you get one?

Types of POA: Generally, there are POAs for financial decisions and separate ones for health and welfare decisions. A "lasting power of attorney" (LPA) in the UK, for example, is set up while you still have mental capacity and comes into effect if you lose that capacity (or earlier if you choose for financial LPAs). Different jurisdictions have different names (e.g., "durable power of attorney" in the US), but the principle is similar.

Choosing your attorney(s): This is a crucial decision. You need to appoint someone (or more than one person) you trust implicitly to act in your best interests. This could be a spouse, adult child, sibling or a trusted friend. Consider their financial acumen (for financial POAs), their understanding of your values, and their willingness and ability to take on the responsibility.

Where do you go? While there are some DIY kits available, due to the legal significance and potential for misuse if not drafted correctly, it's highly recommended to use a solicitor or attorney specializing in estate planning or elder law. They can advise you on the right type of POA for your needs, ensure it's tailored to your specific circumstances, explain all the implications and make sure it's legally valid according to your local jurisdiction.

What to expect: The process involves discussing your wishes, formally appointing your attorney(s) and outlining the scope of their powers. The document must be signed by you (the donor), your chosen attorney(s) and witnesses, and in many places (like the UK for LPAs), it needs to be registered with a public body (e.g., the Office of the Public Guardian in the UK) to be valid. This registration process can take several weeks or even months, so it's vital not to leave it until it's urgently needed.

Cost: Using a solicitor will involve legal fees, which can vary. However, this cost is often a small price to pay for the immense security and peace of mind it provides, and it's typically far less than the potential costs and stress of your family having to apply for a court order if you lose capacity without a POA in place.

So, take the time to put a POA in place. It's the difference between chaos and control, between panic and preparation. Make the call, understand your options, sign the papers and secure your legacy of care and foresight. Because the smartest move you'll ever make is to prepare for what you can't always see coming. Don't wait for a crisis.

Beyond the legal documents

You've spent your life building your wealth, cultivating your values and crafting your unique story. But I know your legacy isn't just about the numbers left in an account. It's intrinsically woven into the people you love, the principles you embody and the lasting mark you hope to leave on the world. Yet, when it comes to actually passing down that legacy, we enter the deeply human, often messy and unpredictable territory of family dynamics.

The transfer of wealth from one generation to the next is rarely a simple transaction. It's a potent moment where long-buried family dynamics can suddenly erupt, dormant sibling rivalries can flare, unspoken cultural expectations can clash and carefully guarded secrets might finally surface. Even the most meticulously crafted estate plan, technically perfect on paper, can unravel in an instant when raw emotions and unresolved relational baggage enter the picture.

When it comes to legacy planning, it's vital to recognize that it's not just about assets; it's profoundly about principles and people

Family dynamics are just as crucial as financial planning. You see, toxic patterns don't just exist in boardrooms; they can thrive within families too, often subtly undermining even the best intentions. So, when it comes to legacy planning, it's vital to recognize that it's not just about assets; it's profoundly about principles and people. Your true inheritance shouldn't just be financial capital, it must include the values you instill – integrity, responsibility, collaboration, generosity and open communication. Family harmony, built on these foundations, acts as a powerful multiplier effect for wealth, amplifying abundance and well-being when there's mutual respect and a shared willingness to address conflicts head-on with love and understanding.

This brings us to a critical point, often avoided due to discomfort. The importance of open communication within the family before a crisis hits or an inheritance is distributed. Don't let unresolved issues fester, especially those involving money or differing expectations. They act like energetic blockages, disrupting the healthy flow of your intended legacy. Dealing with them directly, however challenging, fosters the understanding and collaboration necessary for wealth to resonate positively through generations.

Initiating these conversations requires courage and sensitivity. Consider saying to your parents (if applicable and appropriate), siblings or adult children:

- "I've been thinking about the future and the legacy I want to build, and I'd love to understand your perspective and share mine. Could we set aside some time to talk about our family values around money and responsibility?"
- "It's important to me that we're all on the same page regarding expectations for the future. Can we talk openly about hopes, fears and how we can best support each other?"
- "I'm working on my estate plan, and clarity is really important to me to avoid any future misunderstandings. Could we discuss how best to ensure fairness and honour everyone's contributions and needs?"

Approach these discussions with curiosity, empathy and a genuine desire to understand different viewpoints. It's not about dictating terms but about co-creating clarity and minimizing the potential for future conflict. When family aligns, wealth doesn't just grow; it resonates with shared understanding and purpose.

The dark shadow side of inheritance

We love to romanticize inheritance money. The opportunities it might fund, the dreams it could unlock, the security it promises. But there's a shadow side we rarely talk about. Handled insensitively, inheritance can become corrosive, a force that fractures families and leaves scars that may never heal. The psychology behind these challenges is far more complex than we'd like to admit.

Money, at its core, often symbolizes security, freedom and even love or validation. But for some, the introduction of significant inherited wealth can trigger deep-seated insecurities, feelings of inadequacy, resentment or a perceived sense of unfairness. When these raw emotions surface, they can create a volatile breeding ground for conflict.

Take the all-too-common story of siblings who were once inseparable, until an inheritance dispute erupts and shatters that bond forever. A lifetime of shared memories becomes tragically overshadowed by resentment, entitlement or perceived slights. Lawsuits are filed. Families are divided. Relationships are destroyed. Often, it's rarely about the money itself, but about what it represents – love, validation, acknowledgment. When people feel undervalued or overlooked in the process, the inheritance, meant as a gift, can feel like a final judgement or even become a weapon used to exert control. It's a tragic irony that unfolds in countless families, leaving lasting pain.

The flip side is the "golden cage" of inherited wealth. Imagine a young adult handed a vast fortune they didn't earn. Instead of freedom, they can find themselves trapped. Potentially disconnected from personal ambition, lacking a driving purpose and struggling with a fragile sense of self-worth because they've never had the satisfaction of building something

> Wealth without purpose or skill can become a double-edged sword

themselves. They may have never learned essential skills in managing money because it was always just there. The very thing that should have empowered them can become a perceived curse, sometimes leading to apathy, lack of direction, strained relationships or difficulty finding intrinsic motivation. This phenomenon, sometimes dubbed "affluenza", highlights the burden unearned wealth can sometimes bestow, the potential guilt of having without deserving, the erosion of motivation and the isolation that can come from living in a perceived bubble. Left unaddressed, it can hinder personal growth and lead to profound unhappiness, demonstrating how wealth without purpose or skill can become a double-edged sword.

If you need proof of how a lack of planning can create chaos even around monumental success, consider the widely reported story of the music icon Prince. Known for his meticulous artistic control and visionary independence, he stunned the world when he passed away unexpectedly in 2016 without a will. Despite leaving behind an estate initially valued at hundreds of millions of dollars, including invaluable music rights and unreleased recordings, his failure to leave clear instructions meant his legacy was immediately thrown into uncertainty. Minnesota's intestacy laws dictated that his estate would pass to his sister and five half-siblings, regardless of what his personal wishes might have been. What followed was a complex and costly six-year legal battle involving valuation disputes (the IRS initially valued the estate much higher than the administrators), challenges from potential heirs and disagreements among the confirmed siblings on how to manage and distribute the vast assets. Millions were spent on legal and administrative fees, draining significant value from the estate and delaying the eventual settlement. Prince, a man who fiercely controlled his creative output during his life, ultimately lost all control over his legacy after his death, leaving behind not just incredible music, but also a cautionary tale about the crucial importance of proactive estate planning.

The lesson here is that no amount of money or sophisticated legal strategy after the fact can fully override the chaos caused by a lack of prior planning or deep-seated family dynamics. Inheritance planning without consciously addressing the human element beforehand is like building a magnificent mansion on quicksand. It's only a matter of time before the foundations become unstable.

The bright light of inheritance

But it absolutely doesn't have to end this way. Wealth, when handled with intention, communication and aligned values, can be an incredibly powerful force for healing and unity. It can serve as a catalyst for reconciliation and positive change. I've witnessed families previously torn apart by bitterness find ways to come together to honour a thoughtfully constructed legacy.

Imagine two estranged sisters, divided for years over a failed business venture. When their father passes away, he leaves his estate structured in a way that gently forces collaboration, perhaps through a trust requiring joint decisions. To access the funds, they have to communicate, find common ground and act as a team. It's undeniably uncomfortable at first, fraught with old wounds. But slowly, through the shared task and perhaps guided facilitation, they begin to rediscover their bond. The inheritance becomes not just a financial gain but an unexpected bridge back to each other.

Or consider the granddaughter inheriting a significant sum from her grandmother, a woman who always deeply regretted not having the opportunity to pursue higher education. Instead of simply absorbing the funds, the granddaughter establishes a scholarship fund in her grandmother's name, providing transformative opportunities to young women who lack the resources for college. In doing so, she turns her inherited wealth into a living legacy, one that honours her grandmother's values and aspirations. This is your legacy in the making. Your wealth, properly wielded and mindfully planned, echoing positively through generations. It's the soul of your story, the essence of your values and the fire of your impact continuing to burn brightly long after you're gone.

The urgency of now

My children aren't just receiving an allowance; they're already learning the foundations of building their own empires, even from the age of seven. Why? Because the tipping point for intentional legacy creation is NOW. This isn't some distant goal or vague vision to attend to "someday", it's a living, breathing reality that demands your full attention today. Warren Buffett's philosophy consistently highlights the "time value of planning". The undeniable truth that proactive decisions made now multiply their positive impact exponentially later. Joe Vitale speaks powerfully about "seizing momentum", capturing the potent energy of the present moment to accelerate your desired future. You're either consciously sprinting toward your vision, or you risk losing precious ground to inertia and circumstance.

Your legacy is about far more than transferring assets; it's about passing down a mindset. Your heirs won't just inherit your wealth; they'll inherit you – your values, your resilience, your wisdom. The legacy you'll leave is being formed right now, moment by moment, choice by choice. Every investment, every boundary, every values-led decision you make now is a brick in the foundation of the life you're building. And make no mistake, this life is yours to design. This isn't about chasing more for the sake of it; it's about more meaning, more alignment, more life. The world won't pause until you feel ready to have that difficult conversation or do the "boring" yet essential admin. Readiness isn't a prerequisite; it's a decision. My hope, my invitation, is that you take everything within this chapter – the tools, the shifts, the love – and use them boldly. Start where you are, move with intention and build something so deeply aligned it holds forever.

CHAPTER 9
LEGACY IN MOTION

So far, we've explored the essential tools for building and preserving your wealth, but let's be brutally honest, your legacy is about far more than money. It's about the people you love, the values you embody and the indelible mark you leave on the world. And that demands conscious choices.

You didn't get here alone. Every financial decision you've made, every risk you've taken, every moment of hesitation or bold calculation has sent ripples through the lives of those who will come after you, shaping their opportunities and their very understanding of what's possible. Your legacy is not a passive inheritance; it's a story written in the lives of your descendants and the generations to come, a narrative they will carry forward, for better or for worse.

That's why this isn't just about avoiding probate or minimizing taxes. It's about ensuring that the values you hold most dear – your work ethic, your compassion, your commitment to justice – become the guiding principles for future generations. It's about equipping your heirs, not just with financial resources, but with the wisdom, the character and the moral compass they need to navigate their own journeys with integrity and purpose.

Think of the stories that will be told about you long after you're gone. Will they speak of a life lived with intention, a fortune used to uplift and empower, a legacy of positive change that continues to resonate through the lives of those you cherished most? Or will they whisper of squandered opportunities, of bitter disputes, of a fortune that divided rather than united? The choice, ultimately, is yours.

Consider the enduring impact of families like Ford, whose innovations revolutionized industry, or Rothschild & Co., whose financial acumen shaped markets and nations, their wealth seeding philanthropic ventures that continue to extend their influence today. Think of the Grosvenor family, whose strategic stewardship of assets has built a dynasty with profound and lasting impact. This powerful chapter is not about hoarding your wealth; it's your signal for crafting a legacy that's both significant and sustainable.

I know you're the type of person who refuses to let their impact fizzle into obscurity. Your manifesto is one that architects enduring influence; you're a visionary who understands that true prosperity isn't measured by the numbers on a balance sheet but by the magnitude of the legacy you engineer. Because wealth without purpose-driven impact is nothing more than an unfinished symphony, a masterpiece left unpainted, a story without an ending. Every choice you make is scripting the financial playbook for those who come next: your children, your nieces, your nephews. They're watching, absorbing and modelling the way they will navigate their own wealth. You're either architecting a dynasty or leaving them a tangled mess of survival-mode thinking. This is the moment, the turning point, the chapter where you fortify your unshakable financial ecosystem. One that breeds influence, power and enduring prosperity. This is about building a dynasty that doesn't just withstand time but commands respect across industries, boardrooms and history itself. To build that, you need brutal honesty.

Family and fortune

If your financial strategy is built on outdated ideals and you're clinging to some polished, picture-perfect fantasy of legacy, you're already losing the game. As we've explored, family isn't static and it's not a tidy, airbrushed portrait. It's blended, fractured, chosen, extended. It's filled with tensions, unspoken truths and power dynamics that determine who holds the keys to influence. If you ignore these realities – the people you inadvertently exclude, the wounds you choose not to see – the legacy crumbles. These are the cracks that will bring it all crashing down. We're not here to build a brittle fortune that dissolves within a generation; we're here to construct an empire. A force so solid that it outlives you, outgrows you and becomes something far greater than you ever imagined. This is your financial legacy. It's time to design it with intention, strategy and relentless clarity.

So, let's sharpen the mission that fuels this financial empire. The real question isn't just what is your wealth for, but what will it do? Yes, what a powerful question indeed! Will it stand as an unbreakable pillar of generational power, a fortress of prosperity that shields and elevates your lineage for centuries, accessible and relatable not just to the financial elite but to anyone aspiring to build a secure future for their loved ones? Will it be a force that bends history, funding revolutions of thought, industry and humanity itself? Or is it the ultimate currency of freedom, the ability to move, to choose, to design life on your own uncompromising terms? Because we know that wealth is more than a number; it's leverage, it's power. It's the ability to turn the impossible into the inevitable. It's the key that unlocks doors others never even knew existed, the instrument that dismantles barriers, rewrites the rules and reshapes the world in our vision. You've made it to this critical intersection, and your journey so far has undoubtedly shown you that commanding wealth means wielding it with purpose, precision and unstoppable intent. We're building assets and forging a dynasty of visionaries, architects and disruptors who refuse to accept the status quo. We're the catalyst for transformation, the force that drives

Commanding wealth means wielding it with purpose, precision and unstoppable intent progress, justice and innovation. And now, we move from vision to execution, from strategy to leading, from intention to unstoppable impact.

Turning purpose into power: the mechanics of a living legacy

The next generation won't simply inherit your wealth; they will be forged to command it. This isn't left to chance, but cultivated through deliberate, powerful learning opportunities. Establish a junior investment board for younger family members, empowering them with a modest sum to manage under your strategic guidance. Involve them directly in philanthropic decisions, tasking them with researching charities and presenting their cases with conviction. This is why we're laser-focused on becoming financial titans, architects of wealth, strategists of influence, and builders of an empire that does more than sustain; it disrupts, innovates and reshapes industries. Wealth isn't a safety net; it's a weapon, a force of nature that multiplies under the stewardship of those disciplined enough to master its flow.

This isn't about playing by existing rules; it's about rewriting them to serve your grand vision. We track, measure and recalibrate with laser precision, like a general assessing the battlefield. Every asset is a tool, every decision a chess move in the grand game of power. Wealth moves; it compounds; it bends reality under the force of your intent. And giving? That's not mere charity; it's a calculated act of strategic influence. Identify causes that align with your family's core values and invest in them in a way that creates tangible, measurable impact. Imagine funding a scholarship for underprivileged students in a field your family champions, or establishing a foundation that tackles a specific societal issue. This is a ripple effect engineered to create waves that reshape the world. Success isn't just profit; it's impact. It's the lives transformed, the barriers dismantled, the future rewritten in our image. Witness the Bill & Melinda Gates Foundation, relentlessly tackling global health and education, or the Ford Foundation's enduring commitment to democratic values and poverty reduction. These are not just powerful examples of wealth; they are blueprints for strategic influence, legacies of lasting global change.

Defining your non-negotiable family code

Take a moment to reflect and articulate: what are the three to five core values that your family's wealth must uphold and promote? For each value, brainstorm one concrete action or investment that would bring it to life. This isn't just an intellectual exercise, it's the beginning of your family's guiding constitution. Invest only where your deepest convictions align. Allocate resources with the precision of a master strategist, ensuring every move, every investment, drives you closer to unstoppable momentum, in a way that feels authentic and achievable for your unique circumstances. And don't raise passive recipients of fortune; cultivate power players who own their financial destiny. From the moment they can grasp the concept of value, they're immersed in its mastery; not as spectators, but as tacticians, testing strategies, making moves and commanding wealth as second nature.

This active involvement is crucial because money isn't just currency; it's kinetic power, energy in motion. It's the current that drives opportunity, fuels innovation and shapes the next era of leadership. By allowing future generations to engage with wealth constructively, they understand its potential beyond mere accumulation; they see it as a tool for creation and impact, connecting their actions to broader outcomes. Wealth isn't created by waiting; it's summoned by action. Influence isn't maintained; it's multiplied through strategic engagement. This is how dynasties are built, and this is how your wealth is immortalized, becoming an unstoppable force for generations.

Leading by example: the true inheritance

A legacy isn't just about passing down wealth; it's about instilling wisdom, shaping character and engineering a mindset that commands financial sovereignty. And that starts early, in the everyday moments. For my eldest daughter, Chloë, the journey began with investment accounts set up in her name, automated contributions ensuring steady growth, and quarterly "strategy meetings" where we review her portfolio together, using age-appropriate language. She doesn't just hear about investing; she experiences it firsthand. We research companies before we invest. Simple things, like choosing brands she knows, connecting effort to reward as she uses earnings from household chores to fund her own stock purchases. The lesson here is foundational – wealth isn't won; it's built with patience, intention and discipline.

But financial education alone isn't enough, because the most powerful inheritance isn't money; it's identity. As Dr Gabor Maté so brilliantly states, our children don't just inherit our assets, they inherit our emotional wiring. They absorb how we handle stress, how we navigate abundance, how we show up in the world. Wealth isn't just about numbers; it's about energy. And if that energy is laced with fear, scarcity or shame, it doesn't matter how much money we pass down, because that scarcity mindset will unravel it faster than any market crash ever could.

I saw this firsthand in my own home. My mother loved designer clothes, but guilt wrapped itself around every purchase like an iron chain. She would hide new outfits in her wardrobe, stashing them away as if she were concealing some great transgression. Spending was always a point of tension, a whispered source of conflict. That unspoken lesson was that enjoying wealth was somehow wrong, and that landed squarely in my subconscious. For years, I carried that programming like an invisible weight. If I was gifted something beautiful, I wouldn't use it; I would save it "for best". I had luxury makeup sets that sat untouched, stunning clothes with the tags still on, waiting for some undefined "perfect" occasion that never came. It wasn't about being practical; it was scarcity masquerading as wisdom. Scarcity doesn't just whisper in your ear, it infects the way you move through the world. Wealth is meant to be lived, experienced, activated.

If we lead with fear, our children will shrink in hesitation. If we lead with shame, they'll second-guess their own worthiness. If we teach them that abundance is something to hoard, to tiptoe around, to hide, then they'll never learn to command it with confidence. But if we embody security, purpose and a healthy relationship with wealth, that becomes their inheritance. They'll walk into boardrooms with presence. They'll make decisions with conviction. They'll use what they have instead of letting it gather dust. Legacy isn't just about what you leave behind, it's about what you normalize. And the most powerful thing we can normalize for the next generation is sovereignty – over their wealth, their choices and their power to shape the world. And that starts with you. Right here. Right now. This isn't about what we say, it's about what we demonstrate. Kids don't follow instructions; they follow examples. That's why the most powerful legacy move isn't just crafting airtight financial structures, it's becoming the person we want the next generation to model. Wealth without wisdom leads to decline. Wealth with wisdom creates dynasties. This is how legacies are engineered, not just through assets, but through alignment, through the transmission of principles that empower future generations not just to maintain wealth, but to expand it, to own their destiny, to build something that outlasts us all.

> The most powerful thing we can normalize for the next generation is sovereignty – over their wealth, their choices and their power to shape the world

Beyond your bloodlines

What if your vision for legacy extends beyond direct descendants, or if you don't have children? The principles of legacy remain potent. Your "heirs" can be mentees, promising young talents or even organizations whose missions align with your values. Consider establishing a foundation, a scholarship or a named endowment that continues to fund the causes or develop the talents you care about. This strategic philanthropy becomes a powerful way to ensure your influence and values endure. This approach connects directly to earlier discussions on wills and estate planning (as detailed in Chapter 8), where you define not just what you leave, but to whom and for what purpose, ensuring your resources continue to work toward your vision long after you're gone. The key is intentionality in identifying those individuals or entities who will carry the torch of your legacy forward.

Empowering young entrepreneurs

True empowerment is about ownership, showing the next generation that wealth isn't something they passively inherit; it's something they create, command and expand with intention. As I say this out loud, it gives me goosebumps to know that in today's world, we are empowered to change a whole line of our heritage. That's why, in our family, we don't just talk about money; we activate it. We expose our children to the reality that wealth isn't built in a single stream; it flows in multiple directions, through diverse ventures, ideas and investments. And the earlier they grasp this, the sooner they unlock the mindset that will serve them for life.

Chloë got her first taste of entrepreneurship not as a bystander, but as a co-creator. She didn't just witness the launch of my first limited company, Dream Catcher Innovations Ltd, she named it! From developing a children's journal to contributing to YouTube videos, she learned the power of her voice, the weight of her ideas and the impact of meaningful self-expression. She didn't just see wealth being built, she was inside the process. And that's the key – involvement. We nurture her small business ideas not as "cute" projects, but as legitimate ventures, discussing target markets, pricing and marketing in simple terms. She sees firsthand that wealth isn't just grown through investment but through innovation, creativity and relentless execution. She earns her pocket money, she suggests new ways that she'd like to make money, and where she wants to contribute to how our household runs. In time, her little sister will have the same autonomy.

Can you see how this isn't just about financial literacy; it's about financial agency? When the people around you understand they have the power to create value, they cultivate something far greater than a strong bank balance; they develop self-efficacy. They stop seeing wealth as something handed down and start seeing it as something they architect for themselves. This mindset doesn't just shape their relationship with money; it shapes the way they navigate life itself. It influences their decisions on education, careers, risk-taking and innovation. It fosters resilience in an unpredictable economy. It transforms them from passive participants in the financial system into strategic players who move with purpose, conviction and clarity. And that's how legacies are not just maintained, but multiplied.

Intentional giving

Giving isn't an afterthought; it isn't a checkbox on a moral to-do list. It's your ultimate power move, because true abundance is about both accumulation and circulation. Money, like energy, stagnates when hoarded and thrives when it flows with purpose. That's why integrating charitable giving into our family's philosophy isn't some feel-good side note; it's a cornerstone. From early on, Chloë and Ophelia are learning that wealth is not a prerequisite for impact. You don't need millions to make a difference; you need intention.

Whether it's donating a portion of their pocket money, choosing causes that ignite their passion (like an animal shelter or a local food bank), or engaging in hands-on acts of service like volunteering time, they see that even the smallest contributions can create ripples of change. This isn't about fulfilling an obligation, it's about ownership. It's about shaping the world we want to build.

And here's some magic for you; generosity is a multiplier, not merely a nice-to-have or a polite afterthought. It's a non-negotiable imperative, woven into the very fabric of our financial architecture. We don't just plan to give; we engineer a self-sustaining engine for transformational impact. Wealth isn't a personal possession; it's a global catalyst. And when wielded with audacious precision, it doesn't just ripple; it reverberates across generations. Every act of giving, whether it's wealth, time or influence, has a way of coming back in unexpected, powerful ways. The more we put into the world, the more expansion we create, the more relationships we build, the more impact we generate. Giving is about amplification. It strengthens communities, fuels innovation, and accelerates exciting opportunities far beyond what we could ever predict. Real wealth isn't measured by what we keep; it's measured by what we create.

Your legacy strategy

The time for passive contemplation is over; this is your summons to architect an enduring dynasty. Your immediate strategy begins with **architecting a 100-Year Plan.** Dare to project your vision far beyond your own horizon. Ask yourself: what indelible impact will your family name carry a century from now? Which core values must be the unwavering bedrock against shifting market tides and societal transformations? Envision the future you're truly engineering for your descendants; not merely their financial standing, but the significance of their contribution to the world.

With this century-long vision as your North Star, the next imperative is to **construct your Family Code.** This isn't about etching rigid, unbreakable rules in stone that stifle dynamism; it's about forging a written constitution – a clear, potent framework of core principles and ethical guidelines. This document becomes the blueprint for ensuring your legacy is built upon unwavering integrity and profound purpose, designed to be adaptable in its strategies yet utterly constant in its foundational tenets.

To animate this code and vision, you must **form your Dynasty Council.** This is the engine room for intergenerational collaboration, decisive decision-making and continuous strategic education. Whether formal or semi-formal, this council will be instrumental in cultivating future leaders within your lineage, navigating conflicts with constructive resolve, and ensuring every action remains fiercely aligned with your long-term mission, recalibrating tactics as the landscape evolves but always championing the core vision.

Critically, this dynasty is fuelled by **empowering the next generation.** This isn't a task for later; it begins the moment they can grasp fundamental concepts. Immerse your heirs in age-appropriate, dynamic discussions and tangible activities surrounding wealth, strategic finance and impactful philanthropy. Don't just tell them; involve them. Grant them real-world experience through active participation in family investments or business ventures. Provide robust mentorship, whether from your own experience or trusted advisors, and crucially, give them the autonomy to sharpen their financial acumen and ignite their entrepreneurial spirit, always within the guiding ethical framework of your Family Code.

Finally, understand that a legacy is not a static monument but a living, breathing entity that demands **commitment to continuous evolution and rigorous evaluation.** To ensure its unstoppable growth and enduring relevance, you must embed processes for regular, honest assessment and strategic adaptation. What are you measuring? Track the hard metrics:

the financial expansion of legacy assets, the quantifiable impact of philanthropic endeavours – scholarships funded, community projects brought to fruition. But also gauge the engagement of younger generations in steering the family's financial direction and their unwavering adherence to the Family Code. And what are you adapting to? The answer is everything: external economic earthquakes, disruptive technological advancements, evolving societal needs and the internal dynamics of your own growing family – new members, shifting aspirations. The ultimate objective is an impact that doesn't just endure but amplifies, constantly evolving as a vibrant, undeniable force for good.

Your legacy will not be a footnote of chance; it will be the headline of a meticulously constructed masterpiece – an undeniable testament to your vision, your values and your fervent commitment to forging a future that screams your highest aspirations. Step into your destiny. Ignite the momentum. And empower the next generation to not just continue what you started, but to amplify it into an echo that reshapes the world.

Now your blueprint is drawn and your vision is clear. The momentum is yours for the seizing. But empires aren't built on blueprints alone; they are forged through decisive action. The difference between a dormant dream and a living dynasty is the courage to make the first move, right now. Forget waiting for the perfect conditions; perfection is the enemy of progress. Your legacy demands action, not contemplation.

Operation legacy launch – your Zero Hour

Enough strategy. Enough talk. Dynasties aren't dreamed into existence; they're launched with decisive force. Scan the battlefield imperatives we just mapped: architecting the 100-Year Plan, forging the Family Code, assembling the Dynasty Council, weaponizing the next generation's potential, committing to relentless evolution. Or pinpoint any other legacy-defining strike ignited within you. Now, lock onto ONE breakthrough action. The single, concrete move you will execute to detonate progress on your legacy within the next seven days.

Maybe it's commandeering the calendars for that first 100-Year Plan summit. Perhaps it's hammering out the defiant opening clause of your Family Code. It could be identifying and recruiting the first powerhouse member of your Dynasty Council. Or maybe it's initiating the first shock-and-awe investment deposit for an heir, or finally executing that high-stakes, crucial family conversation on wealth and values.

Seize your pen. Command your keyboard.

Right now. No hesitation.

Etch that **ONE ACTION** into existence. Define it with ruthless precision. Ask yourself:

- What is the clear **objective**?
- What is the non-negotiable **deadline**?
- What is the absolute first **tactical step**?

For instance, your defined action might look like:

- "Launch siblings comms: draft Family Code summit invite – execute by Tuesday EOD".
- "Intel gather: research top three family foundation advisors – recon complete Thursday 17:00".
- "Blueprint genesis: outline core values for 100-Year Plan – mission accomplished Saturday AM".

This is your Zero Hour. This is the moment inertia shatters, where raw intention explodes into untouchable kinetic force. This single, decisive action executed now is the first tremor of the empire you're building. Stop consuming information about legacy – go conquer it. The countdown starts now. Execute.

CHAPTER 10

IGNITING YOUR CONSTELLATION

Look at you. Just take a moment to see how far you've come. I'm proud of you. Feel the power pulsing within you, the undeniable shift from where you started to who you are right now. You've journeyed through the often-turbulent inner landscapes of your own money story, faced down the shadows of scarcity and doubt and emerged not just intact, but utterly transformed.

Now doesn't that feel SO good! That quiet hesitation that once held you back? Obliterated. Replaced by a laser focus, a bold resolve and a deeper understanding of wealth not just as accumulation, but as energy – potent fuel for your freedom, your purpose, your most audacious dreams.

You've done the deep work. You've not only architected your Evergreen Wealth Engine (Chapter 5) for sustainable prosperity but aligned every financial decision with the core values driving your most authentic, magnificent life. You've stepped into your power, forging your Ikonic brand, becoming that Magnet for More Money (Chapter 6) that draws opportunity toward you rather than endlessly chasing it. You're building your wealth; you've become its master, reclaiming your power and designing systems for sustainable freedom. You've built your personal fortress, secured your foundation, claimed your financial sovereignty. You're standing tall, powerful, equipped. Celebrate yourself for a minute. You've earned it.

Here's my electrifying truth for you: the journey doesn't end here. In fact, this incredible foundation you've meticulously built is just the start. It's your launchpad for your greatest impact yet. Having mastered the art of generating and managing wealth for yourself and your loved ones, we arrive at the final, most expansive frontier. Extending your abundance, that power, that light outward. This chapter is the culmination, where we explore the profound principle that wealth achieves its highest potential, its most vibrant expression, not when hoarded, but when shared and strategically circulated.

Wealth achieves its highest potential, its most vibrant expression, not when hoarded, but when shared and strategically circulated

Think of a single, brilliant star. Beautiful, yes. But a constellation? That illuminates the entire sky. We're moving from building your star to igniting your constellation. This is where true fulfilment lies, where your legacy transcends personal achievement and becomes a living force for positive change. In this final chapter, we dive into the art and strategy of amplifying your impact through your community. We'll explore how to leverage the incredible resources you now command. Your money, yes, but also your time, your influence, your network, your unique genius, to uplift others, foster connection and create powerful ripples of shared prosperity. This is about moving beyond *More Money, More Life* for you, and stepping into architecting *More Money, More Life* impact for everyone your journey touches. So, let's get started.

Why community is your ultimate investment

You've architected your financial fortress, secured your engine and built your money magnet. The numbers are starting to move, the foundation is solid. But let me ask you this: what's the point of a magnificent castle if you're the only one rattling around inside its walls?

What is community in the *More Money, More Life* context? Community is any ecosystem where you feel energized, connected and compelled to contribute. It could be geographic (your neighbourhood), passion-based (your creative collective, your environmental cause), professional (your industry titans, your founder network), values-aligned (your online tribe) or philanthropic (the mission burning in your soul). It's where your energy finds resonance.

There's a profound truth often whispered but rarely shouted; wealth accumulated solely for oneself eventually hits a ceiling of fulfilment. It can feel strangely isolating, a summit reached alone, leaving you wondering, "Is this all there is?" I recognize that echo from my own past, standing inside a successful corporate career, earning good money, yet feeling deeply unfulfilled, and startlingly lonely. We're wired for connection, for contribution, for belonging. Locking away your resources, however vast, can inadvertently lock you away from the very richness of human experience that true wealth is meant to unlock.

This is where the magic of community comes in, revealing wealth not as a finite resource to be guarded, but as an expansive energy designed to circulate and multiply. Think about it; investing in your community, whether through sharing your knowledge, your time, your connections or your capital, isn't depletion, it's activation. It unleashes a powerful multiplier effect. Imagine a single, thriving plant in a pot versus a lush, interconnected garden ecosystem. In the garden, roots intertwine, nutrients are shared, pollinators buzz between blooms, creating a resilience and vibrancy far exceeding what any single plant could achieve alone. Sharing resources within a community creates exponential returns. Unexpected collaborations spark, shared knowledge accelerates growth for everyone, mutual support provides resilience during challenges, and collective problem-solving achieves breakthroughs individuals couldn't manage on their own. When the tide rises in your community, all boats lift, including yours.

More profoundly, engaging with your community becomes the ultimate expression of your purpose. Remember the core values, the driving vision you unearthed earlier in this journey? Using your wealth as a tool to empower others, to contribute to causes that resonate with your soul, to help build the kind of world you want to live in, this is where your financial success transcends the balance sheet and becomes deeply, intrinsically meaningful. It's no longer just about "more money"; it's about channelling that money to fuel "more life", not just for you, but for the collective. It's the highest alignment of your resources with your reason for being here.

And in doing so, you begin to cultivate perhaps the most valuable, yet often overlooked, asset of all. Social capital. This isn't measured in pounds or dollars, but in the depth and quality of your relationships, the trust you've earned, the strength of your network built on genuine connection and mutual support. Financial capital can buy many things, but it cannot buy authentic belonging, loyalty or the spontaneous opportunities that arise from a community that knows, likes, trusts and champions you. Think of the founder who gets crucial, honest feedback from trusted peers in their network before a major pitch, saving them from a costly mistake. That's social capital in action. Or the connection made at a community event that leads to an unexpected dream collaboration years later. This social capital becomes your ultimate safety net, your richest resource, unlocking doors and creating possibilities that money alone simply cannot reach. Investing in community isn't just philanthropy; it's the shrewdest investment you can make in a truly resilient and abundantly supported life.

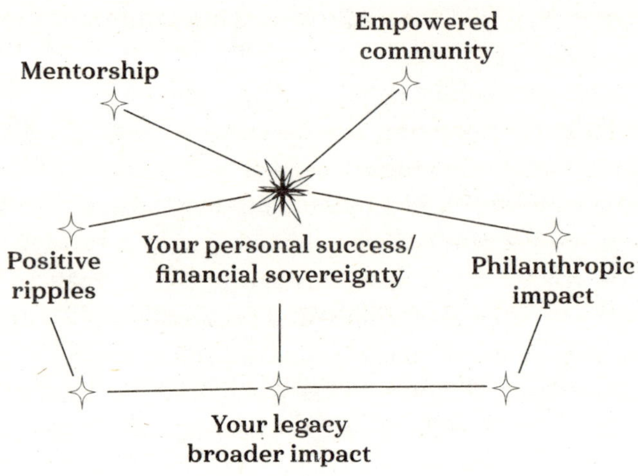

Igniting your constellation

Where and how to make your mark

Alright, the "why" of community investment is blazing within you. You get it! This is giving back and amplifying your life, your wealth, your impact. You feel that undeniable pull, that simmering desire to share the potent abundance you've cultivated. But desire without direction is just diffused energy. The crucial next strike is translating that internal fire into focused, external demolition of the old paradigms and the construction of your new reality. It's time to move from purpose to pinpoint precision. It's about identifying where your unique energy will not just contribute, but command attention and create seismic shifts.

It's time to deploy your inner compass and pinpoint the communities where your presence will be nothing short of revolutionary

So let's harness that power. Where will you make your stand? Where will your unique energy ignite the most significant impact? This isn't about obligation or where you think you should be; this is about strategic, soul-aligned action. It's time to deploy your inner compass and pinpoint the communities where your presence will be nothing short of revolutionary.

Your resonance radar

This exercise is your reconnaissance mission into your own energetic landscape, pinpointing the specific ecosystems where your unique genius will not only be welcomed but will actively thrive and multiply. Grab your journal, dedicate some uninterrupted time, and let's chart your impact zones.

For up to three potential communities that instinctively come to mind or pique your interest, it's time to delve deep. Be ruthlessly honest; this is about authentic connection, not wishful thinking.

First, for each potential ecosystem, **identify and describe it**. What's its name or how would you describe it (e.g., "The Female Founders Network", "Future Corporate Leaders", "Global Innovators for Sustainable Tech Mastermind")? Get specific. What **category** does it fall into – is it geographic, passion-based, professional, values-aligned, philanthropic or a hybrid?

Next, explore the **energetic pull** – your **Why This, Why Now?** What specifically draws you to this ecosystem? Is it a shared audacious vision, a gut-level alignment with their core values, an urgent problem they're solving that ignites your fire, or a profound sense of belonging? Describe that magnetic pull. Then conduct an **energy check**. On a scale of 1 (drained) to 10 (absolutely electrified!), how intensely energized do you feel right now when you think about engaging with this community? If it's not at least a 7, seriously question its fit.

Then, consider your unique ignition point. What are your initial thoughts on your potential impact here? How might your genius manifest? Does your strategic mind see a gap you could help fill? Could your network open crucial doors? Do your specific skills – be it marketing, finance, leadership or tech – address an obvious need? How could you uniquely fuel their fire? And critically, does the thought of contributing in this way, to this community, make you feel a resounding "HELL YES!" deep in your core? This feeling is non-negotiable.

Finally, uncover your deep connection, why this ecosystem matters to your soul. Beyond logic, what's the deeper, perhaps unspoken, reason this community resonates with your personal journey, your story, your soul's purpose? What part of you truly comes alive when you imagine being part of it? This is where true, sustainable commitment is born.

This is about uncovering the authentic channels for your most powerful contributions. Let your intuition, that finely tuned inner compass we've been honing, guide you. You might identify one core ecosystem that demands your primary focus, or perhaps two or three where you can make distinct, meaningful impacts.

Trust the resonance. When your energy aligns powerfully with a community's purpose, you don't just find a place to contribute; you find a launchpad for your most amplified self. This clarity is the bedrock upon which you'll build your strategy for truly impactful engagement, ensuring that where you plant your seeds, you cultivate not just growth, but a legacy.

Uncovering your contribution style

Once you have a sense of *where* your energy wants to flow, connecting you to communities that genuinely resonate, the next vital step is defining *how* you can show up most powerfully and authentically. But knowing where to make your mark isn't enough; the real alchemy happens when you discover your unique contribution style.

While strategic financial support is absolutely a potent tool for change, we must shatter the limiting belief that donating money is the only, or even primary, way to make a significant difference. The truth, the one that aligns perfectly with the journey you've been on throughout this book, is that your greatest, most impactful and most fulfilling contribution often flows directly from your signature power. It lies in leveraging the skills you've painstakingly honed, the wisdom you've earned through experience, the passions that ignite your soul and the resources you now command, including the influence from the incredible brand you've built. This isn't about finding just any way to give back; it's about discovering how to contribute in a way that's a natural extension of who you are, tapping into your core strengths and values. Contributing in this aligned way isn't just more impactful for the community; it's exponentially more energizing and fulfilling for YOU, preventing the burnout that comes from obligation and allowing you to give generously from a place of genuine strength and joy.

Unlock your impact signature

Let's unlock how you're uniquely designed to contribute. Grab your journal. Rapidly answer:

1 What activities/skills make me feel instantly energized and "in the flow"?
2 What problems in the world (or my community) genuinely fire me up or break my heart?
3 If I could offer ONE non-financial gift to uplift others right now, what would it be?
4 What compliments do I receive about my natural talents or way of being? Don't overthink, capture the raw energy. This is the blueprint of your most authentic, signature power that's your unique contribution style.

So, let's explore the rich palette of possibilities beyond the bank account, guided by your signature power:

Mentorship and knowledge sharing: You've navigated challenges, achieved success and learned invaluable lessons. Sharing that wisdom, guiding those walking a similar path just behind you, is an incredibly potent form of contribution. Mentorship taps into our fundamental need for guidance and validation. For the mentee, having someone believe in them, share shortcuts and normalize challenges can radically accelerate their growth and self-belief. For the mentor, it reinforces their own expertise, provides profound fulfilment through generativity (contributing to the next generation) and creates a legacy of knowledge transfer. It's a high-impact exchange of wisdom and potential.

Skill-based volunteering: Consider offering your hard-earned professional talents – that sharp marketing savvy, your financial acumen, strategic planning prowess or tech skills – to organizations or individuals who desperately need them but may lack the resources. For me, this often manifests as coaching and mentoring. Perhaps it's because my signature power is to care deeply and listen intently. Over my career, I've had the privilege of mentoring hundreds of people, often simply for the joy of it. Honestly, witnessing that spark ignite in someone else is single-handedly one of the most rewarding experiences imaginable. So often, people seek guidance when they're navigating a tough transition, feeling utterly stuck, or facing a challenge that seems insurmountable. Yet sometimes all it takes is a single hour of focused conversation, of truly being heard, seen and understood, to unlock something profound within them. You witness the relief wash over their face, the dawning of clarity, the flicker of courage strengthening as they find the resolve to go out and finally do the thing! That potent impact isn't limited to coaching; think about your unique professional gifts and the powerful shifts they could create.

Creating opportunities: Use your platform, your business, your network to intentionally open doors for others. This could mean hiring diverse talent (as I've been privileged to do in my own business through partnerships like the one with the Ian Karten Charitable Trust, an amazing organization dedicated to helping disabled people achieve independence and employment through technology training), promoting emerging leaders, making strategic introductions, or creating pathways for those often overlooked.

Convening and connecting: Perhaps your unique genius lies in weaving connections, intuitively seeing the potential synergy between people or ideas that haven't yet converged. If you're that natural connector, recognize this isn't just a personality trait; it's a potent gift for community building. Wield it intentionally. Architect spaces, whether intimate gatherings or dynamic forums, designed to bring the right people together around shared goals. Facilitate the kind of collaborations that spark innovation, host events that deepen relationships, and ignite the conversations that lead to breakthroughs within your community. Your profound reward is witnessing someone take flight, empowered by an introduction you made or a collaboration you sparked. That creates a deeply satisfying ripple effect, a powerful return that money alone can't buy.

Advocacy: Unleash the power of your voice, your influence, your platform. Yes, that Ikonic brand we built! (see pages 141–9). Use it to champion causes you believe in, amplify messages that matter and stand up for others. This could be using your social media platform to champion a local cause, writing to policymakers about an issue you care about, publicly endorsing a colleague for a promotion, or correcting misinformation within your professional network. Sometimes, simply speaking truth or offering vocal support is the most potent contribution you can possibly make. Don't hesitate to step forward when your voice can make a difference. There's a unique strength, a fierce clarity that arises when we advocate for another or for a principle we hold dear. Conversely, the silence of being a bystander when you could have intervened can leave a corrosive echo of regret long after the moment fades. I learned this viscerally years ago when I intervened to prevent someone from being unfairly dismissed. It wasn't comfortable, but acting on conviction felt essential. Knowing that that person's career continued, directly contrasted with the devastating alternative my silence might have permitted, and cemented for me the tangible, life-altering power of advocacy. Your voice has weight; use it.

Aligning your spending and investing with your core values becomes one of the most consistent and potent ways you contribute to collective well-being

Conscious consumption and investment: Don't underestimate the profound impact embedded in your everyday financial choices. Where your money flows truly matters. This is about wielding your financial agency with intention. Choosing to consciously support local businesses bolsters your community's unique identity and economic resilience. Prioritizing ethical suppliers and your local communities actively contributes to fairer labour practices or environmental sustainability. Impact investing – strategically investing in businesses tackling climate change, funding startups focused on accessible healthcare or using platforms directing loans to small businesses in underserved communities – means you're directing your capital toward enterprises explicitly designed to generate positive social or environmental outcomes alongside financial returns. Think of the ripple effect; your choices influence market demand, support livelihoods aligned with your values, and contribute directly to the health and vibrancy of the communities you care about. As you step more fully into your financial power, aligning your spending and investing with your core values becomes one of the most consistent and potent ways you contribute to collective well-being, turning everyday transactions into acts of purposeful change.

Your Authenticity Filter

Now, underpinning all of this is the non-negotiable Authenticity Filter. This is where you align your "where" and "how" with your deepest core values, your unique strengths (your "Zone of Genius"), your passions and, yes, your realistic time availability. Contribution born from obligation or a sense of "should" quickly leads to resentment and burnout. Contribution that flows naturally from who you are, the skills you love using, the causes that genuinely ignite your passion, and the communities where you feel authentic connection becomes a source of immense joy and sustainable energy.

Ask yourself, "What truly electrifies me? What activities leave me feeling energized? Where can I offer my signature power, not just my obligated self?" Running your potential contributions through this filter ensures that giving back doesn't become another task on the to-do list, but rather a fulfilling, integrated and joyful expression of your most authentic, abundant self. This is how you make your mark in a way that is both impactful and sustainable.

Your energetic alignment audit

Before committing your precious energy and your valuable time, run opportunities through this rapid audit:

1 **Values check:** Does this deeply align with my core values (list your top three)?
2 **Genius zone:** Does it leverage skills I LOVE using?
3 **Excitement level:** On a scale of 1–10, how genuinely excited (not obligated) does this make me feel?
4 **Energy drain risk:** Realistically, can I commit the required time/energy without hitting burnout? Be ruthlessly honest. Only proceed with opportunities that score high on alignment, excitement and energetic sustainability. This ensures your contribution fuels you as much as it helps others.

Leveraging your Ikonic brand

Yes! Your mission critical intel has been acquired. Your resonant communities are targeted, your signature power primed for authentic contribution. Brilliant. Now we hit the ignition. We're moving from dormant potential to decisive, kinetic impact. It's time to unleash your full arsenal – your influence, your financial clout, your irreplaceable time, your relentless energy – with strategy, not just well-meaning generosity. Your objective is to amplify your positive impact to an unprecedented scale, rewriting what's possible.

First, let's talk about leveraging your Ikonic brand for good. Remember that powerful magnet, that undeniable presence you meticulously crafted? That influence isn't just for attracting clients or opportunities for you; it's a potent force multiplier for causes and communities you care about. Intentionally deploy your assets – your visibility, your credibility, the compelling narrative you command. Use your platform to champion initiatives that need a spotlight. Lend your influential voice to amplify messages that deserve to be heard. Step up and lead community efforts where your expertise can make a tangible difference. Perhaps offer to serve on the board or as a Trustee for a non-profit whose mission ignites your passion, host a fundraising event leveraging your network, or become a spokesperson for a campaign aligned with your values. Your influence is capital – deploy it. This isn't about diluting your brand; it's about elevating it, demonstrating that true leadership uses its power responsibly and purposefully to lift others.

Strategic generosity

Consider your era of scattered, reactive donations obliterated. Your generosity now becomes a high-impact instrument in your financial portfolio, engineered to be deployed with the same precision and intent as your wealth-building strategies. I don't mean creating cumbersome complexity;

it's philanthropy architected for potent, measurable results that ripple outward.

1 **Define your focus:** What specific change fuels your passion (e.g., youth literacy, animal welfare, clean water access)? Get laser-focused.
2 **Research and align:** Identify organizations whose values resonate and who demonstrate tangible results (check their impact reports, ask questions).
3 **Choose your strategy:** Decide between one-off high-impact gifts or sustained multi-year support for deeper change.
4 **Consider beyond cash:** Could your skills, network or platform amplify your financial gift? Integrate your unique contribution style. This strategic approach transforms your financial generosity from a simple transaction into a targeted investment in the future you wish to help create.

Crucially, let's focus on the potency of empowerment in your contributions. While direct aid definitely has an important place, the most sustainable and affirming generosity often focuses on building capacity within others, rather than fostering dependency. Think "teaching someone to fish" versus simply giving them a fish. Are you funding skills training that equips someone for long-term success, or just providing a temporary fix? Are you mentoring an emerging leader, sharing your knowledge and network to help them soar, or are you inadvertently doing the work for them? Prioritize contribution models that provide tools, skills, access and opportunities, empowering individuals and communities to build their own sustainable futures. For example, instead of just donating food, support a programme that teaches sustainable farming techniques and provides micro-loans for tools. Instead of just giving cash, fund a coding bootcamp that equips individuals with high-demand job skills. This is generosity that truly transforms. Because when individuals gain tangible skills, something profound ignites within them. Confidence. That confidence fuels bolder action, builds resilience and often inspires them to pay it forward, mentoring others coming up behind them. That beautiful ripple effect, that multiplication of empowerment, THAT is the true magic.

Finally, underpinning all strategic impact is the continuous cultivation of connection. Building strong, authentic relationships is the invisible architecture of thriving communities. Move beyond transactional networking and commit to genuine connection. Practise deep listening, truly hearing the needs and aspirations of those around you. Show up consistently, not just when you need something. Authentically celebrate the successes of others within your community – their win is a collective win! Offer help proactively, share resources freely and build trust through reliable, values-aligned action. It's these seemingly small, consistent acts of connection that weave the strong, resilient fabric of a supportive ecosystem where everyone can thrive.

Move beyond transactional networking and commit to genuine connection

The echo of your life

As we weave together the threads of strategic generosity and authentic connection, we arrive at the profound heart of the matter. The enduring echo your life creates. We've moved beyond the mechanics of wealth generation and even the strategies of giving back, into the realm of legacy. But let's redefine that word, liberating it from the narrow confines of purely financial inheritance or business accolades. Your true, most resonant legacy isn't just etched in wills or corporate histories; it's imprinted on the hearts and fabric of the communities you touch. It's measured in the lives uplifted, the opportunities sparked, the positive change catalysed because you chose to engage, to share, to contribute.

Ask yourself not just, "What will I leave behind?" but "How will the community be tangibly better, more vibrant, more hopeful because I walked this path?" Consider Grace, a successful graphic designer who felt disconnected. She started offering pro-bono branding workshops for local startups in her "Zone of Genius". Years later, her town boasts a thriving small business scene, many crediting Grace's early guidance and the collaborative network she fostered as the spark. Her legacy isn't just her portfolio; it's woven into the economic vitality of her entire community. This community imprint may well become the most meaningful chapter in your entire story.

> Your true, most resonant legacy isn't just etched in wills or corporate histories; it's imprinted on the hearts and fabric of the communities you touch

Now, let's talk ROI (return on investment) on your strategic community engagement, but banish from your mind the sterile thoughts of dividends or typical capital gains. The true yield we're chasing here isn't quantifiable on any spreadsheet; we're igniting something far more primal – a tidal wave of profound joy, the bedrock of deep, authentic fulfilment. For too long, a toxic narrative has been ruthlessly peddled, that contribution is mere duty, a grudging sacrifice that inevitably drains your precious reserves. We're not here to politely question that fallacy. We're here to detonate it. To obliterate it. Because the truth you're about to embody is infinitely more electrifying.

When you unleash your signature power – that fierce, authentic force at your core – with pinpoint alignment and raw, unadulterated purpose, and you witness its direct, tangible ignition in the lives of others … that's not "giving back", that's unleashing an explosion of meaning. That's tapping into an unparalleled surge of pure, visceral joy. It's not a depletion of your hard-won resources. This is undiluted rocket fuel for your spirit. This visceral, intrinsic reward, this deep, resonant knowing that you're a potent force for positive change is the undiluted essence of *More Life, More Money* that money alone, locked away in a vault, can never, ever purchase. It's the soul-fire that ignites your momentum, making every future step more powerful, more resonant, more you.

Your acts of generosity and empowerment are rarely isolated sparks; like potent seeds planted in fertile ground, they're intrinsically designed to create self-perpetuating cycles of abundance. When you foster collaboration within a community, you build trust and social capital that enables future collective action. Your contribution becomes a pebble dropped in a still pond, sending out ripples that inspire others, build bridges, strengthen the ecosystem and, ultimately, foster greater prosperity and well-being for everyone. Imagine mentoring one promising young entrepreneur; they succeed, hire locally, then mentor others themselves, creating jobs and fostering innovation far beyond your initial interaction. That's the amplified return on empowering contribution. You become a catalyst not just for individual change, but for cultivating a more supportive, generative environment all around you.

Understanding this power, witnessing these ripples, calls you into your highest role yet; a conscious steward of the resources you command. It's an empowered responsibility, a privilege earned through your journey. It's about embracing the understanding that the wealth, influence and platform you've built are potent tools to be wielded wisely, intentionally and generously for collective upliftment. It's about consciously choosing to direct your power toward building the kind of equitable, supportive and thriving communities you wish to see in the world. Stepping into stewardship is the ultimate expression of your financial mastery and your purpose-driven life, transforming your success into a force for enduring good.

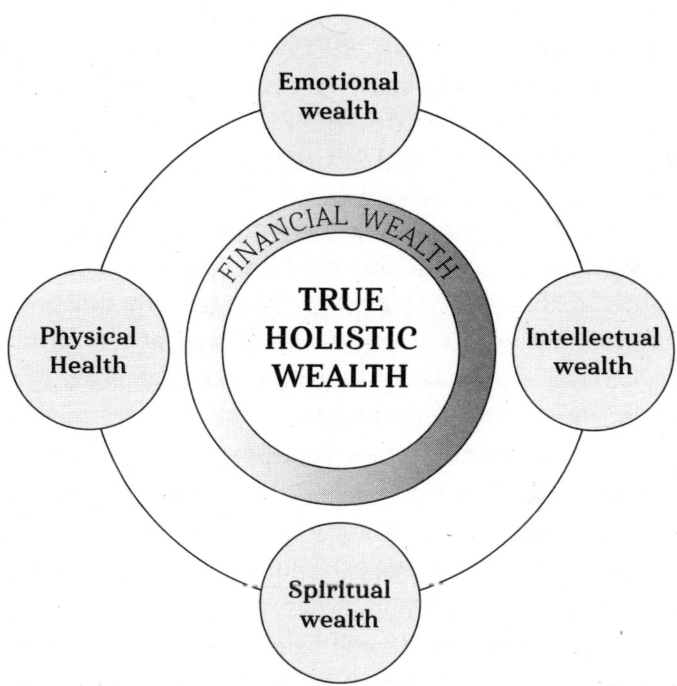

This is true holistic wealth

More Money, More Life

And so, we arrive not at an ending, but at a magnificent new beginning. Look back for a moment at the path you've carved with courage and intention.

First, you plunged inward, confronting the tangled landscapes of your personal money story, obliterating limiting beliefs and rewriting the narratives that once held you captive (Awareness). From that reclaimed territory, you forged potent Alignment, defining your solid purpose, architecting your formidable Evergreen Wealth Engine, and igniting your Ikonic brand, that irresistible Magnet for More Money. Then, you unleashed decisive Action: executing your vision with precision, fortifying your legacy for those you love and seizing your role as a conscious steward, amplifying your impact throughout the vibrant ecosystem of your community. You haven't just changed; you've fundamentally revolutionized your relationship with wealth, hardwiring it to your deepest values and highest vision. This is the full circle.

So, what now? You hold far more than new financial skills or a bigger bank account. You hold the operating system for a redefined reality. You are the *More Money, More Life* promise in motion. Because authentic wealth was never about the money. It was always about integration. The alchemy of your purpose with your prosperity, your financial command fused with soulful fulfilment. This is your power: to fund audacious dreams, to fuel relentless waves of change. This is your freedom: to live boldly, give generously, be unapologetically you, etching your indelible mark on the world by unleashing your true self.

You didn't just finish a book; you ignited your internal code. The arsenal is yours – a revolutionary mindset, deeply embedded. A blueprint, boldly drawn. This moment isn't just a new chapter; it's an ignition point, unleashing exponential expansion, embodied mastery and impact that reverberates.

So, architect your future. Step forth. Command your destiny. Not as a mere builder of wealth, but as the visionary, the conscious, formidable force for good you've become. Deploy your resources, your platform, your resonant voice, your signature brilliance, not just to rise, but to elevate.

The world isn't just hoping for your brilliance. It's waiting. It needs what only you can bring, fully unleashed. Live with fierce intention. Lead with audacious courage. Give with strategic power. And forge that magnificent, enduring legacy.

More Money.

More Life.

More Impact.

REFERENCES

Chapter 1

Yehuda, R, & Bierer, L M (2009), "The Relevance of Epigenetics to PTSD: Implications for the DSMV", *Journal of Traumatic Stress*, 22(5), 427–434. https://doi.org/10.1002/jts.20448

Maté G, *When the Body Says No: The Cost of Hidden Stress,* Vermillion, 2019

Chapter 5

McKinsey & Company, "Don't Let the Pandemic Set Back Gender Equality", *Harvard Business Review*, September 2020

Chapter 7

Skinner, B F, *The Behaviour of Organisms: An Experimental Analysis*, New York: Appleton-Century-Crofts, 1938

Wolpe, J , *Psychotherapy by Reciprocal Inhibition*, Stanford, CA: Stanford University Press, 1958

Dweck, C S, *Mindset: The New Psychology of Success*, Random House, 2007

Clear, J, *Atomic Habits*, Random House, 2021

Chapter 8

Ferriss, T, *The 4-Hour Workweek: Escape the 9–5, Live Anywhere, and Join the New Rich,* Vermillion, 2011

Erikson, E H, *Childhood and Society*, W W Norton & Company, 1950

Vitale, J, *The Attractor Factor: 5 Easy Steps for Creating Wealth (or Anything Else) From the Inside Out*, Wiley, 2005

Chapter 9

Maté, G, *The Myth Of Normal: Trauma, Illness And Healing In A Toxic Culture*, Vermillion, 2002

ABOUT THE AUTHOR

Hi, I'm Sarah, authority builder, personal branding strategist and unapologetic champion of leaders who refuse to blend in.

I help brilliant minds become visible forces, turning quiet expertise into undeniable authority. If you're ready to stop blending in and start becoming unignorable, you're in the right place.

I earned my stripes in the toughest arenas – Wall Street and the City of London. There, I didn't just survive – I learned to lead with integrity, navigate power and reinvent myself without waiting for permission. As Global Head of Conduct and Ethics for a FTSE100 firm, I learned what few titles teach: real leadership isn't a position; it's a choice. It's the courage to set the standard, the conviction to build trust from the inside out, and the audacity to lead out loud – even when the room expects you to shrink.

Launching Ikonology meant channelling that edge and insight into the IKONIC™ Framework: The Architecture of Undeniable Authority:

- **Impactful-driven identity** Define your unique category of one. Stop competing and start crafting a powerful narrative that makes you the go-to authority in your field. Your identity becomes your magnet – drawing in ideal clients and making competition irrelevant.
- **Knowledge-driven credibility engine** Build a fortress of trust and expertise. Establish your authority through strategic podcast placements, a dominant presence on platforms like LinkedIn, and thought leadership that shapes industry conversations – so choosing you is the only logical choice.

- **Opportunity erchitecture** Become the signal, not the noise. Engineer your network to create strategic collisions; surround yourself with collaborators, referral partners and media, positioning you at the centre of the industry's most important conversations.
- **Narrative power** Your story is the currency of human connection. Weave your origin, expertise and bold vision into a compelling narrative that resonates deeply, transforming you from another expert to an unforgettable guide for your audience.
- **Influence at scale** Achieve omnipresence with intention. Repurpose your core message across the right channels, meeting your ideal audience wherever they already gather. Influence isn't about shouting louder – it's about strategic presence that compounds your impact.
- **Consistency that converts** Forge your legacy through relentless consistency. Develop sustainable systems and workflows to show up with boldness, building compounding trust and momentum that ensures your brand works for you – day in, day out, for decades to come.

By executing each pillar, you become irreplaceable, unignorable and in-demand – the architect of your own authority, impact, and legacy. The IKONIC system is not about chasing every opportunity – it's about magnetising the right ones, so you move from being a choice to becoming the choice in your niche.

Final word

The biggest lever you'll ever pull is your own decision to take action. No more waiting. No more hiding. No more playing small.

Raise your voice. Bank your worth. Live your legend.
More Money. More Life. More Impact.

RESOURCES

Accelerate your brand and life

Let *More Money, More Life* spark you, then fuel your growth with these field-tested favourites:

Mindset and psychology

Turn to these books if you feel like your mindset is holding you back from the success you deserve.

- Hossel, M, *The Psychology of Money*, Harriman House, 2020
- Sincero, J, *You Are a Badass at Making Money*, Viking, 2017
- Hill, N, *Think and Grow Rich*, The Ralston Society, 1937

Wealth building and investing

Turn to these books if you want to understand the fundamentals of building long-term wealth, from creating passive income to making smart investment decisions.

- Collins, JL, *The Simple Path to Wealth*, JL Collins LLC, 2016
- Dunlap, T, *Financial Feminist*, HarperCollins, 2023
- Graham, B, *The Intelligent Investor*, Harper & Brothers, 1949
- Kaur, S, *Girls That Invest*, W. F. Howes, 2022
- Kiyosaki, R, *Rich Dad Poor Dad*, Plata Publishing, 1997
- Tu, V, *Rich AF*, Penguin Random House, 2023

Habits and execution

Turn to these books if you need to build powerful, consistent habits and a strategic framework for turning your ambitions into reality.

- Clear, J, *Atomic Habits*, Avery, 2018
- Covey, C, McChesney, C, & Hewling, J, *The Four Disciplines of Execution*, Free Press, 2012

Influence and authority

Turn to these books if you want to become the go-to expert in your field, and to build a brand that attracts opportunities instead of chases them.

- Miller, D, *Building a StoryBrand*, HarperCollins Leadership, 2017
- Cialdini, R, *Influence: The Psychology of Persuasion*, Harper Business, 1984

Next-level platforms and communities

UK Financial Literacy MoneyHelper, Citizens Advice
US Financial Literacy Investopedia, Consumer Financial Protection Bureau
Entrepreneurship SCORE (US), Enterprise Nation (UK)
Personal Branding LinkedIn Learning

Tools and apps

Turn to these resources if you need to connect with the right people, find crucial support, and get the tactical knowledge to expand your influence.

- **Budgeting** YNAB, Mint, Monzo, Starling, Personal Capital
- **Investing** Vanguard, Fidelity, Interactive Brokers, Hargreaves Lansdown (UK)

Keep building your legacy with Sarah

- **Ikonology© Agency** – where bold voices become Ikonic brands: www.ikonology.co.uk
- **Sarah's blog** Deep dives into wealth, visibility and fearless leadership: sarahbennettnash.com/blog
- **Speaking events** Upcoming live dates and speaking topics: sarahbennettnash.com/speaking
- **LinkedIn** Fresh thinking, daily truth and nonstop brand fuel: linkedin.com/in/sarahbennettnash/

The only asset no one can take from you is the one you build from the inside out. Make your brand unforgettable, let it be the reason they say your name long after you've left the room.

ACKNOWLEDGEMENTS

Writing this book wasn't just a project, it was evolution in real time. From foggy early ideas to fierce conviction on every page, I've been bolstered by a wildly supportive circle.

To Chris Graham – thank you for being a brilliant sounding board, even through the tears and turbulence.

To my sister and my ride-or-die crew (you know who you are!) – thank you for standing in my corner, always. Your faith gave me the courage to keep showing up, even when it was hard.

To my incredible daughters, Chloë and Ophelia – thank you for the laughter in the chaos, the hugs in the meltdowns, and that fierce "Go for it, Mummy!" battle cry that powered every late-night sprint and dawn brainstorm. Your love is my launchpad, my true legacy, and my greatest fuel. Never forget, you are the reason I reached for possibility, and the living proof that faith in your dreams is always worth it.

To Team Ikonology, past and present, you are more than colleagues; you are the backbone of of this mission. You turned vision into movement and never blinked when I pushed it to ten.

To my mentors and wise guides, your questions and high standards made me braver and sharper. For believing in my unwritten chapters before I did, thank you.

To my early readers, your directness, passion and critical eyes made this book what it is. You called out my verbosity, and I love you for it.

To Kizzy, the expert in turning dreams into ink-and-paper reality. And to my editor, Sophie, you're the secret force behind this landing just right. To the powerhouse team at

Watkins Publishing your vision and boldness brought this message to shelves. Thank you.

And you, bold reader, you showed up. You chose growth over comfort, substance over safe. May the chapters ahead launch you into your own version of *More Money, More Life.*

INDEX

Note: page numbers in **bold** refer to diagrams.